The Libidinal Economy of China

The Libidinal Economy of China

Gender, Nationalism, and Consumer Culture

Perry Johansson

LEXINGTON BOOKS
Lanham • Boulder • New York • London

Published by Lexington Books
An imprint of The Rowman & Littlefield Publishing Group, Inc.
4501 Forbes Boulevard, Suite 200, Lanham, Maryland 20706
www.rowman.com

Unit A, Whitacre Mews, 26-34 Stannary Street, London SE11 4AB

British Library Cataloguing in Publication Information Available

Library of Congress Cataloging-in-Publication Data

Vig, Perry Johansson, 1963– author.
The libidinal economy of China : gender, nationalism, and consumer culture / Perry Johansson Vig.
pages cm
Includes bibliographical references and index.
ISBN 978-0-7391-9262-7 (cloth : alk. paper) — ISBN 978-0-7391-9263-4 (electronic)
1. Consumption (Economics)—Social aspects—China—History. 2. Consumers—China—History. 3. Sex—China—History. 4. Sex role—China—History. 5. Feminine beauty (Aesthetics)—China—History. I. Title.
HC430.C6V54 2015
306.30951—dc23
2015027755

⊗ The paper used in this publication meets the minimum requirements of American National Standard for Information Sciences—Permanence of Paper for Printed Library Materials, ANSI/NISO Z39.48-1992.

Printed in the United States of America

Contents

Acknowledgments

Some of the following chapters have a prehistory as conference presentations, book chapters, and articles. Chapter 2 was published in an earlier version as "Selling the New Chinese Woman: Consumer Culture and the Chinese Politics of Beauty" in *Images of the "Modern Woman" in Asia: Global Media, Local Meanings,* Curzon Press, 2001, 94–123, edited by Shoma Munshi following an IIAS conference in Leiden. It was also presented at a panel on women's magazines at an Association for Asian Studies conference in Washington. Chapter 3 was in an earlier version published as "The Cultural Politics of Fashion: Chinese Sartorial Regimes and the Magazine *Elle*" in *Stockholm Journal of East Asian Studies*, vol. 16, 2006. Chapter 4 began as a European Association for Chinese Studies conference presentation in Barcelona that *China Information* wanted for a special edition on the body (September 1998, 13: 59–84). It appeared as "White Skin, Large Breasts: Chinese Beauty Product Advertising as Cultural Discourse." Chapter 5 was accepted by the journal *Postcolonial Studies* as "Consuming the Other: The Fetish of the Western Woman in Chinese Advertising and Popular Culture" (Volume 2, Issue 3, 1999, 377–88). Still earlier versions had been presented at the Media in Asia conference held at Hong Kong University and at an AAS meeting in Chicago. Chapter 6 was discussed at the conference "The Nations Two Bodies: Aesthetic Figurations of the Political" arranged at Luxemburg University and published in German by Oliver Kohns and Martin Doll (eds.) *Perspektiven der politischen Ästhetik*, Wilhelm: Fink, 2015, as "Die libidinöse Ökonomie Chinas."

I want to thank Jean Olson for doing a fine job editing the manuscript; the many-headed team at Lexington Books for hard work and believing in the book, and the two anonymous peer reviewers. The book is dedicated to my loving children for putting up with a writing father and for giving me so much inspiration, love, and joy.

Introduction

> Do you want our Chinese women? We can give you ten million.
>
> —Mao Zedong to Henry Kissinger[1]

The objective of this book is twofold. First it wants to describe from a psychoanalytical point of view some of the desires and anxieties of contemporary Chinese nationalism as it evolved after the 1989 student protests and crackdown. In order to do so we focus on a hitherto underexplored archive: the discourse on gender, sex, and the body of the emerging Chinese consumer culture of the 1990s. Serving noticeably as a metaphor for the broader society and modernization, the female body has throughout the twentieth century been a conduit for a multitude of expectations and fears. Now we examine its meaning and uses as economic reforms geared up and the former social fabric tore apart.

The second aspiration behind this study has been unwrapping China's convoluted relationship with its Occidental Other, describing what we perceive as a Western Gaze and its role in organizing an essential part of China's self-image. The underlying theme for our investigation is therefore the postcolonial remnants of a certain sexual geopolitics now challenged by an economically, technologically, and militarily rising China. Domestic aspirations here mix with what has been described as an international complex of "racial castration" to discursively restructure fantasies of a particular Chinese femininity together with a simultaneously fearful sexual desire for the Western Other.

In this introductory chapter we first provide a short theoretical discussion on the nature of consumer culture before proceeding to describe certain sociocultural aspects of China's economic reforms, including how the official campaign on patriotism morphed with the changing media landscape to create, for the first time, a truly widespread nationalism.

CULTURE AND CONSUMPTION

Anthropologist Grant McCracken claimed in his 1988 book *Culture and Consumption*, "The consumer revolution is now seen to have changed Western concepts of time, space, society, the individual, the family and the state."[2] Other scholars have equated Western modernity and consumer culture. Sociologist Don Slater, for example, argues, "Consumer culture is in important respects *the* culture of the modern West."[3] Conflating Western modernity with consumer culture, these scholars focus not primarily on the consumption of goods but on the consumption of meaning.[4] For them, consumer culture is a visual culture in which images dominate, making consumption a production of identity and dreams. As British sociologist Mike Featherstone writes, "Consumer culture offers productive consumption in the sense that it holds out the promise of a beautiful and fulfilling life: the achievement of individuality through the transformation of Self and lifestyle."[5]

Much historiography has the Self and individuality appearing the very first time with the advent of modern consumer culture. Colin Campbell, for example, traces the ethics of consumption back to nineteenth-century Romanticism and its notions of the Self. He argues that modern hedonism is characterized by a longing to experience in reality pleasures conceived of in daydreaming and that consumption, advertising, and marketing all satisfy and cannibalize these desires.[6] The modern hedonist, Campbell argues, is a daydreamer who is able to control himself and his emotions. He projects his fantasies onto an object, something he can buy. The modern hedonist is furthermore able to imagine that the acquisition of this product will bring certain experiences. Consumption, as Campbell sees it, expresses the romantic's wish to change and become someone else. The new patterns of consumption, he concludes, are the cause and, at the same time, the consequence of these romantic definitions of the Self.

Others pinpoint the origin of modern consumer culture in the 1920s, and instead of giving primacy to culture and mentality, they concentrate on the political economy, showing how new modes of mass production, mass consumption, and marketing led to changes in values and mentality. Historian Stuart Ewen suggests that the creation of modern, scientific advertising techniques was the engine that created a consumer culture. In the 1920s capitalist crisis of overproduction and underconsumption, modern advertising managed to reduce the time products circulated between production and consumption. The focus of ads shifted, away from the product advertised and toward the consumer. Richard Pollay showed in a broad study of twentieth-century America that advertising content started to change in the 1920s from an "informational" to a "transformational" mode. While earlier ads tried to tell the consumer about the product's characteristics, a new type of ad sought to alter consumer attitudes toward brands, expenditure patterns, and lifestyles.[7]

Marketing techniques such as advertising now emerged as an important element of the economy and became an integral part of everyday life.

In Stuart Ewen's view, advertising not only solved a crisis of capitalism, but it joined with business to radically transform early twentieth-century man. The belief was that a new hedonist ethic would in and of itself bring about a mass consumer market. Ewen cites the claims of advertising industry representatives of the time that they were striving to "break down the barriers of individual habits . . . to superimpose new conceptions of individual attainment and community desire."[8] The advertising business aspired to become, as stated in the title of Ewen's book, the "captains of consciousness." Since advertising assisted in abolishing traditional, puritan values of frugality, moderation, and restraint, it was presented as an effective means by which to create not only a new breed of consumers but a whole new mentality. Thus people were led in the 1920s to give up their traditionally frugal values and to replace them with a new discourse that centered on hedonism and individualism.

In a later text, Stuart and Elisabeth Ewen point to three phenomena they believe played a crucial role in the formation of American consumer culture: Hollywood and its stars, ready-made fashion, and advertising.[9] By providing people with close-up images of the world's most beautiful actors, Hollywood played a role in creating a whole new libidinal economy. The advent of the first mass-produced fashion, prêt-à-porter, enabled more people to dress up and look attractive. Popular forms of media such as women's, fashion, film, and fan magazines contributed to this trend. These new media supplied images, descriptions, and advice on how to improve one's looks, physique, and personality. Advertising also focused increasingly on youth, beauty, luxury, and abundance, all of which consumers came to associate with the goods advertised. Featherstone also points to the massive importance of images in contemporary culture, with advertising and popular culture in general supplying people with a plethora of images that stimulate desire.[10] As movies and illustrated magazines spread images of the manifestations of hedonism, such as luxury and beautiful people, throughout the early twentieth century, modern retailers started presenting their merchandise in new and more spectacular ways.[11]

MATERIALISM

Chinese modernity after 1949 followed a much different trajectory with a paradoxically non-Marxist attempt to separate the economy from the culture. Furthermore, following the Soviet example, China's Communist Party (CCP) under Mao Zedong believed a rich and powerful China would best be achieved by investing as much as possible in heavy industry and by spending as little as possible on private consumption. Just as in the Soviet Union, all economic gain was reinvested, with production figures becoming the sole measure of progress. Though "the masses" in propaganda paintings of the time were represented as sharing an abundance of food and goods, this was Socialist Realism, portraying society not as it was but the way it would become when Communism was finally achieved. Production figures were heavily inflated and peasants forced into collectivization. This developmental strategy demanded that the people of China sacrifice their needs and desires for a glorious future utopia but had to be abandoned when it resulted in history's most devastating famine.

In the 1980s, when the global project of Communism was running into challenging troubles forcing reforms, the CCP revalued individual consumption from being just wasteful into a carrot to motivate people to work harder. Former high rates of capital accumulation were lowered in order to increase individual income and consumption. With less investment going to heavy industry, more was routed to agriculture and light consumer industry. The new approach held that with more things to buy, people would become increasingly industrious to earn the money required to buy those things. As this new policy was implemented, the Chinese economy started to grow rapidly.

As focus now shifted toward consumption, enterprises could no longer produce solely for the sake of statistics; they had to start finding buyers for their products as well. And thus, the customer was brought back into the Chinese economy. The Communist leadership had initiated a full turn from the Maoist developmental model, and even during the Anti-Spiritual Pollution Campaign of 1983–1984, individual consumption remained in favor. *People's Daily*, the premier mouthpiece for the Communist Party, argued—with no irony intended—that "Marxist economics tells us that production without consumption lacks a goal."[12] The same *People's Daily* in 1984 criticized those who ignored consumption and advocated instead a new *consumerist* ethic. The traditional wisdom of keeping clothes for nine years—new for three years, old for three, and patched for three—should be abandoned for the common good of the economy.[13]

What followed has often been referred to as a consumer revolution. With per capita consumption growing by an average of 7 percent per year between 1978 and 1990, consumption more than doubled.[14] During the early 1980s, consumption patterns remained fairly uniform with consumers striving to attain the "big three": a TV set, a washing machine, and a refrigerator.[15] In the 1990s, however, segmentation started to appear. A study from 1994 by management consulting firm McKinsey & Co. estimated that China had more than 100 million active consumers (that is, with annual incomes over US $1,000).[16] At the same time, more than 5.3 million households had annual incomes exceeding 50,000 yuan (US $5,747 at the time).[17] These "nouveau riche" constituted a tiny share of the population, but they played an important role in shaping consumer trends. Their expensive lifestyles came to represent a new ideal for the rest of the population.[18] In just a couple of years, shops selling anything ranging from expensive brands of sneakers to exclusive foreign lingerie sprang up, together with Japanese department stores and American fast-food outlets. The fiery economic growth and the formation of new high-income consumer groups in the 1990s led to increasing sales of expensive imported consumer goods. During the first six months of 1993, Japanese exports of camcorders to China, for example, quadrupled while car imports into China grew eightfold.[19]

Amidst all the media attention on consumption, Chinese youth stood out as the main representatives of the new consumerist China. They were frequently portrayed as big consumers. In the 1980s there were descriptions in Chinese media of the "*xiao huangdi*" (the little emperors). These were the first generation of the single-child family after the implementation of the "one child policy" introduced in the early 1980s. Their childhood experiences were far removed from those of their parents. As single children they have had the full attention of not only their parents but also their grandparents. These children seemed to get everything they asked for. They were the first generation to grow up in a culture of consumption. According to various surveys, these children were responsible for a large share of the post-Mao Chinese families' consumption and are found to influence purchases in families to a comparatively high degree.[20] A report from 1993 showed that among urban families, close to half the income was expended on the family's single child.[21] As some of the first one-child-per-family generation grew up and became university students, they were still accused of conspicuous consumption by the Chinese media. While they were called "little emperors" when they were children, they were now referred to as the "new aristocracy" (*xin guizu*).[22] This "new aristocracy" was said to invite friends to expensive dinner parties and entertainment centers. They spent lavishly on brand-name clothes and expensive trainers. In the press these students were often accused of "high consumption" (*gao xiaofei*), spending much more money than their parents could afford.[23]

With foreign-made products on store shelves, and a deliberate attempt by companies to make their corporate identity known, Chinese consumers started to develop more brand consciousness.[24] A highly visible phenomenon in those days was the obsession with *mingpai* (famous brands). Buzzwords in ads were *Zhongguo mingpai* (famous Chinese brand), *shijie mingpai* (world-famous brand) and *Zhongwai mingpai* (famous in both China and the rest of the world). Consumers took *mingpai* very seriously, reading up on the status of different brands. Newsstands displayed thick, colorful magazines and booklets with titles such as "Famous Car Brands," "Famous Watch Brands from All over the World," and the like. At the time, a friend in Beijing showed me his extremely well-thumbed copy of "Famous Brands from All over the World," a magazine that presented information about categories of goods like cosmetics, fashion, and motorbikes, and ranked them on a scale of one to 10—a "Top Ten" of consumer goods.

By the mid-1990s television stations were running daily shows devoted to shopping and consumer goods, and newspapers also started obsessively covering consumption. Among a plethora of new magazines devoted to consumption were titles like *Xiaofeizhe* (*Consumers*), *Xiaofei zhinan* (*Consumption Guide*), *Shangpin shijie* (*The World of Goods*). In Beijing a local evening newspaper named *Shangpin gouwu zhinan* (*Shopping Guide*) was extremely popular. Central Television ran the show *Chanpin da shijie* (*The Great World of Products*), while Guangdong Television had its own version called *Kan xiaofei* (*A Look at Consumption*). These TV shows were not identified as advertising, but their hosts enthusiastically introduced new products, interviewing customers and shopkeepers, and telling viewers where to buy the featured merchandise.

Since the number of people with sufficient purchasing power was still relatively small, this frenzied behavior seemed premature. Marketing researchers, as well as social critics, talk about a "Third World consumerism," in which people are attracted to and indulge in aspects of conspicuous consumption before having invested in enough food, clothing, and shelter.[25] This model explains why consumerism developed as it did in China. Statistics on Chinese consumption patterns from the 1990s indicate that growth in spending on consumer articles outstripped daily necessities. Furthermore, the proportional difference between growth in sales of consumer goods such as color TVs, compared to daily necessities like food and housing, was greater in China than it was in the West or in Japan at similar stages of their economic development.[26]

The return of capitalism in China caused concern about excessive consumerism and the depredation of indigenous culture and values resulting from what appeared to be wholesale Westernization.[27] Huang Ping, a sociologist at the Chinese Academy of Social Sciences, pointed to both wasteful spending and the erosion of indigenous values when he argued that the consumerism of China's newly rich had become synonymous with modernization.[28] People in general and urban youth in particular tended to attach more importance to consumer goods than to traditional values. His conclusion was, "Tradition has, to a certain extent, been replaced by the culture of consumerism," with the risk of "precious" traditional Chinese values being lost. Huang blamed Chinese youth for excessive consumption while also raising concerns about the effects that consumerism had on distinctly Chinese values. And although Huang Ping did not specifically identify it, one of the institutions most often blamed for spreading consumerism as well as for introducing Western values to the rest of the world is, of course, advertising.

REINTRODUCING ADVERTISING

After the Communist takeover of China, advertising agencies that had existed for a short time during the Republic were forced into state ownership or simply shut down.[29] During the Cultural Revolution, advertising as a "practice of capitalist business" (*zibenzhuyi shengyijing*) was strongly condemned and vanished almost totally from the Chinese mainland. However, in January 1979, shortly after the Eleventh Party Congress, advertising suddenly was acceptable again. The new policy was publicized in an article in the Shanghai daily *Wenhuibao*, which argued forcefully in favor of the return of advertising.[30] This politically motivated piece first lamented what a waste it was that Chinese broadcasts of live sporting events did not fill the pauses with commercials. The common perception of advertising in Chinese society at that time as "bragging" (*chui niupi*) and "trickery" (*bai xuetou*) was, according to the article, the fault of Lin Biao and the Gang of Four. The article further stated that, in reality, advertising had contributed strongly to the economic success of Western countries and was something about which China should learn more. The benefits would be manifold: With its vivid pictures, advertising would direct the flow of goods and accelerate consumption. It would help raise the quality of products as well as offer guidance to consumers. It could "tightly link the masses with production." It was, in fact, an "art form for the masses" (*qunzhongxing de yishu*), and outstanding billboard advertisements, "pleasing both the eye and the mind," could furthermore beautify the cities. Even foreign advertising should be accepted since it would bring in foreign currency as well as "broaden the horizons of the masses."[31]

The article ended with a call for Chinese media to start accepting advertisements. Fourteen days later Shanghai Television ran a commercial for a tonic wine, reporting shortly thereafter that its stations would from then on accept advertisements.[32] Newspapers, magazines, and radio stations immediately followed suit, and foreign companies were informed that they could start advertising products in China.[33] The results were overwhelming.

In 1981 only 100 advertising agencies existed in the PRC, 2,000 other organizations were directly involved in advertising and 6,000 people worked in the field. Ten years later 11,123 advertising organizations, agencies, and media departments employed more than 132,000 people.[34] In the first six months of 1994 advertising revenue increased by 74 percent, making it the fastest growing business in China.[35]

Initially, no advertising laws were in place, and authorities were quite permissive. Television advertising had to be reviewed by the Chinese Advertising Administration's review board for "censorship" (*shencha*), while print advertising was not as controlled. Even if a great deal of self-censorship took place, foreign advertising agencies did not complain about ads being killed because of unapproved content.[36] In 1995, when China finally imposed an advertising law, Western marketing research found it "not excessively stringent compared with Hong Kong's and other international codes."[37]

But to legitimate the reappearance of advertising, it was evident that advertising in China could not be the same as in the West. A distinction was made between "socialist advertising" and "capitalist advertising."[38] Not incidentally, advertising in China was perceived as an instrument of communication between producers and consumers in the same way that propaganda transmits information between political leadership and citizens. Chinese consumers also heard repeatedly that advertising was a *scientific* tool necessary for Chinese economic development.[39] Critical voices against the return of advertising appeared with the 1983–84 Anti-Spiritual-Pollution-Campaign but were directed mainly at foreign influences on China's advertising industry.[40] This campaign complained that some ads were too "sexy."[41] The Chinese Advertising Association responded that female images should not automatically be regarded as spiritual pollution and that images promoting a product should be permitted as long as "health and propriety" were stressed.[42]

During this period, foreign ad agencies regarded Chinese consumers as highly unskilled at participating in a free commodity economy. They therefore made their Chinese ads as old-fashioned and simple as possible. Chinese inexperience with advertising, they argued, rendered them unable to understand more sophisticated ads. When Ogilvy and Mather in 1985 spelled out their guidelines for China, they warned: "Interpretation of advertising is extremely literal, and it is not desirable to attempt analogy or humor of any kind. Emphasis should be given to performance, quality and durability."[43] Reports from the 1980s confirm that ads were often kept simple, straightforward, and information-focused. One study found that Chinese ads often just showed the product in its natural setting while ads in ethnically similar Hong Kong employed imagery and atmospherics as well.[44]

Advertising was, however, regarded a bit differently than in the West: it was not looked down upon but instead perceived as fun, good, and aesthetic.[45] Studies found that the Chinese were more susceptible to advertising than people in other countries and that advertising imagery was more instrumental in making a product known than in other countries.[46] Consumer attitudes seemed to mirror the optimistic and utilitarian views of advertising that the Chinese defenders of advertising advanced in the 1980s: Not only was advertising an important guide for consumers, it had, as the *Wenhuibao* editorial then promised, become an "art form for the masses." In little more than 15 years, China had moved from advertising illiteracy to something akin to advertising ecstasy, and foreign companies did not delay to act on that shift.

When the Chinese market opened up in the 1980s, it was a dream come true for big business. Long before average Chinese had the disposable income necessary for such consumption, they were being targeted by transnational advertising agencies as potential consumers of mass media, advertising, and luxury goods. In addition to economic gains, changes to the political regime were expected. An American economics journalist wrote tongue-in-cheek in 1979 about the return of advertising to China: [47]

> Everyone will lust for a TV set to see the commercials for Coke, Geritol, Crest, Efferdent, Ex-Lax, Anacin and Listerine. Advertising, the Chinese will soon find, is addictive. It's our secret weapon. Far better than hydrogen bombs and nuclear submarines.[48]

Multinational corporations such as Coca-Cola and Philip Morris could start advertising their products and as a sign of how the times had changed, city billboards with socialist slogans and pictures of Mao Zedong were replaced by giant ads for Sony and Eastman Kodak.[49] Even the main ideological journal, *Hongqi* (*Red Flag*), embraced the "practices of capitalist business," making its pages available to ads for foreign companies.[50]

Since it was in no small part the desire for a consumer society like that found in the West that brought down Communism in Europe, the reappearance of advertising and commercialism would also challenge China's ruling structure. Now the Communist leadership's tight control over all means of communication was becoming more difficult to uphold. Particularly challenging was the case of television, whose development into a mass medium was concurrent with commercialization. In the 1970s, television still was available only to a minority of the Chinese population, but by the early 1990s it had become the most popular and widespread entertainment provider in China.[51] TV sets had become the fastest-selling consumer item—from some 27 million in 1982, the number rose tenfold to 230 million by 1992, reaching over 80 percent of the population.[52] This meant that even remote corners of China had access to the global flow of information and images.

China Central Television (CCTV), like all local TV stations, had been owned by the Party and funded by the State. With the return of advertising in 1979, television stations started to bring in revenue by selling ad time. As a consequence, TV content also started to change. Already in the early 1980s, some TV stations had deals with American and other foreign broadcasting companies that sought maximum advertising time. Shanghai Television signed a five-year agreement with Lorimar Productions in 1986, allowing the broadcast of 7,500 hours of American television programs like *Falcon Crest*, *Hunter*, and *Alf*. Mickey Mouse and Donald Duck were part of a later deal.[53] CBS and other giant American TV companies pulled off putting *Dynasty* and *Dallas* on the TV screens of Communist China, and received ad revenues to boot.

Since allowing commercials in 1979, television remained the principal medium for advertising in China. Despite functioning in a Communist state, Chinese television quickly turned commercial and by 1994, not more than a fourth of CCTV's expenditures were funded by the central government. In general, advertising paid for as much as 40–70 percent of station costs by then.[54] Mainly as a result of the new commercial climate, the number of Chinese TV stations had risen to 700 by 1995, with an additional 10,000 cable TV channels. Central Television also had to adapt to the competition. The various departments in the organization became responsible for their own budgets and were often willing to bend a few rules in order to make a profit and continue operating.[55] The internationalization of Chinese television made a great leap forward with the launch of the satellite station, Star TV. Chinese who had a satellite dish could now watch BBC World, Star Plus entertainment, MTV Asia, and Prime Sports.[56]

The print media went through a transformation just as dramatic as that of television.[57] In 1992 the government announced that all newspapers and magazines would have to survive on the market or go broke.[58] Following up on that decision, the Central Propaganda Ministry cut all State subsidies to top newspapers, including the dailies that acted as the Party's propaganda organs.[59] Despite the cutbacks, there were more than 2,000 registered daily newspapers in 1996—ten times more than twenty years earlier. Relying on the market meant depending on sales and advertising revenues. The advertising industry in the 1980s preferred spending its money on national newspapers and television, but in the 1990s it became interested in magazines. Demand from advertisers led Chinese and foreign publishers to launch a whole array of advertisement-friendly magazines geared toward the newly rich. These had titles like *Gold*, *Fortune*, *Qitian buzz* (*Seven-Day Buzz*), *Mingchezhi* (*Famous Cars Magazine*), *Elle*, and *Huabao* (*Pictorial*). Chinese magazines in general also changed as their content became more oriented to what the readership wanted to read.

This developing Chinese consumer culture released a hitherto circumscribed private sphere, accommodating discontent about both totalitarianism and scarcity. But with the "Reform and Opening up" came different challenges for the CCP rule.

TO LOVE ONE'S COUNTRY IS TO LOVE THE PARTY

The death of Mao Zedong did more than help the socialist People's Republic of China to strike out on a more consumer-focused economy; it also heralded the dissolution of the imaginary construct of China's international role, pulling it in line with the symbolic order of the world around it. An effective propaganda apparatus and virtual barriers raised around the nation had effectively prevented information of realities in other countries from reaching the eyes and ears of the Chinese people. But by isolating the nation, Mao succeeded in giving the Chinese self-esteem, creating a feeling of being in control of their destiny and on the way to create a strong and powerful nation. The Communist Party thus misled its subjects into believing that they were better off than people in, for example, the United States. With the advent of economic reforms and the Open Door policy, the Chinese were brought back to reality.

The Communist Party still in power had to come up with an explanation of this bleak reality that they had hidden from the people for so long. It could hardly blame Mao since doing so would effectively implicate the Party in the deception and probably decimate its credibility with the people. Instead, after first blaming the Cultural Revolution on the so-called Gang of Four, they reintroduced the victimization discourse that the belligerent Mao had rejected. Post-1989, the West was thus again blamed for China's poverty and underdevelopment—a strategy that also explained why the West was so well-off compared to China. Casting the blame on the outside world, however, also meant that China reassumed its suppressed position. Once again it was at the mercy of others who had stolen from it a former unity of strength and power, and now were trying to constrain it from retaking what rightly belonged to the Chinese. It also fit nicely with a century of Chinese xenophobia directed against the West, exemplified by sporadic, but often violent outbursts that included killing missionaries, attacking diplomatic representations, and boycotting Western goods.

Anthropologist Benedict Anderson explains that a nation is an imaginary entity created by means of *imitative* action by a collective of individuals.[60] That is, the nation itself has no stable identity but consists of mirroring what a nation seems to be, judging from other existing nations. To this description should be added the retroactive, romanticist understanding of how the nation *is* history, the belief that a nation-about-to-be existed already in the first place, so to speak. Returning to our Chinese case, the birth of that imaginary nation starts when modern ideas and technologies arrive with ruthless European traders backed by imperialistic states. It was in the face of this double onslaught—of modern ideas *and* military force—that a new imaginary was first brought about by a middle class culturally steeped in foreign ideas. Slowly identification with what had earlier been the rule of dynastic families shifted to a vision of China as a nation, in *imitation* of the many others with which the former Middle Kingdom now had to coexist.

With this came a romanticist dream of Chinese exceptionalism that would reappear as the resentment for a lost Thing, of enjoyment stolen from the Chinese. In the aftermath of the Opium War the West, as the story goes, with warships, cannons, and opium forced China into the Western symbolic world order of trade and diplomacy. Therefore Chinese nationalism easily cozied up to Lenin's understanding of imperialism as Western capitalism exploiting the whole world in the same way it did its workers at home. And that idea, which was at the forefront of Maoist ideology, also kept China in a limbo between, on the one hand, accepting the world as it was—the international value system, technologies, institutions, and hierarchies—and, on the other, clinging to memories turned into fantasies that formed a *desire* for a particular Chinese universe that had to be preserved and, eventually, reinstated.

So-called "socialism with Chinese characteristics" and "New Confucianism" were latecomers in a series of countless such attempts to keep a Chinese Spirit while adopting Western technology. Talk of regaining "China's rightful place in the world" exemplified the other strategy. This old problematic relationship between nationalist fantasy and the reality of a particular world order remains at the forefront of the libidinal economy of China, bringing forward desires, anxieties, and fears in a political imagination that contemporary institutions of the CCP try to exploit, control, and pacify alternatively.

Leading up to 1989, important segments of the Chinese people showed an obvious desire to dismantle the Communist dictatorship. The capitalist reforms at first seemed to bring about real change also of the social and political system, and after cracking down so brutally on the peaceful demonstrations in Tiananmen Square, the Party could not go back to its socialist ideology. After all, they were in the process of dismantling the very foundation of the socialist base, supplanting it with a market economy that was grounded on individual consumption and offered little in the way of a social security net. To counter the threat of consumerism and foreign ideas eroding the status of the CCP, they now introduced an ideology with some resemblance to that of its former enemy, Chiang Kai-shek and his Nationalist Party. Jiang Zemin thus launched a campaign to tie the survival of the nation by propagating a particular form of nationalism that the CCP labeled "love-the country-ism" (translated by Beijing into English as *patriotism*). The terminology was chosen to separate good nationalism from what the CCP had brandished earlier as fascist ideology. But it also linked semantically to an already accepted ideology, that of the Party as "passionately beloved mother" (*re'ai de muqin*).[61] Referring to "patriotism" instead of "nationalism" was the Party leadership's attempt to sidestep, any connotations of fascism, but also the problematic position of being simultaneously a multiethnic empire *and* a modern Chinese nation.

The general understanding is that nationalism denotes loyalty to the nation, while patriotism is about love of country. Princeton Professor of Politics Maurizio Viroli brings up a late eighteenth-century thinker to explain why patriotism is different from the murderous xenophobia of last-century nationalism.[62] Viroli refers to how in *La vita civile*, Paolo Mattia Doria first explains that love of country is grounded in how our happiness depends on the well-being of the country we live in. A good government, he advises, must be able to transform the citizens' self-love into love of country. Much as the patriotism of the United States is not primarily about history, ethnicity, and language, but about a certain political system, the CCP now hoped to create a similar displacement of love for the political system it represented by calling for people's love of the nation.

In books and articles, at compulsory study groups, on billboards, and in television ads, patriotism was now propagated as an ideology that complemented Chinese socialism. The whole focus of this campaign, conceived a couple of years after the Tiananmen massacre, was on history. Both Deng Xiaoping and Jiang Zemin had come to the conclusion that the reason behind the students' decision to protest was that they did not know what Western-Chinese relations had looked like before liberation.[63] Chinese students, they believed, needed to be reminded how China had been "bullied and humiliated" by the West. This patriotic reeducation campaign was brought into full effect beginning in 1994, implemented at all school levels nationwide with a newly written curriculum. The belief was that such a campaign on nationalism and history was the best means to "defend against the 'peaceful evolution' plot of hostile powers."

The Chinese leaders were clear about how popular the liberal political system of the West had become among educated Chinese during the first decade of the reform period. After 1989 as they needed to direct people's anger away from the Party, they also had to displace this infatuation with the West. Doing this implied, however, bringing back the victim identity that Mao Zedong had done so much to erase. Now the traumatic, humiliating experiences of when China was weak and at the mercy of foreign powers had to be remembered. So the dialectical relationship between imperialist and colonized that Mao had used, following an idea from Lenin, to partly substitute the Marxist struggle between the bourgeoisie and the proletariat, was reintroduced. In the end, this understanding of the world of course followed Hegel's master-slave dialectic.

The Communist Party's somewhat inverted logic held that since the CCP had "saved" China, it was the protector of the nation, and if people turned away from the Party, the nation would be lost. Loving your country therefore became the same as loving the Party. China's libidinal clockwork was thus reset in the mid-1990s in order to continually regenerate an already existing order. However, the dialectical outcome of the developing consumer culture with this new ideological regime was disquieting.

COMMERCIAL NATIONALISM

Marxist education should have taught the CCP leadership that in a market society the Communist party could not dictate the superstructure of ideology. In hoping that consumer culture would coexist well with State-centered nationalism, the CCP had missed the fact that a capitalist mode of production, with all its particular technologies, also carries its own ideology. As consumer culture brought about a commercialized print media culture in a relatively short time, Chinese media content changed. But most important, the conditions for Chinese media changed. Distribution improved, and magazines and newspapers responded to popular demand to gain readership and sales. This new media landscape set forth also the preconditions for a populist nationalism fueled by, but not restricted to, the "love-the-country-ism" decided on. The authorities therefore had to intervene to stop public and popular demonstrations like when tens of thousands of people protesting the United States' bombings of Belgrade besieged the American embassy in Beijing, while others tried to burn down the Guangzhou consulate. In these and many similar instances during the 1990s, passions ran high and often risked spiraling out of control. Since the organizers used new technologies of mobile phones and text messaging to assemble quickly for protests, they became difficult, even for the CCP, to rein in.

Despite some official angst, however, the two trends of official patriotism and popular nationalism functioned quite well in tandem. "Love-the-country-ism" also cemented an identity that had not been there before. Following Ernest Gellner's ideas, Zhang Xudong argues that it was through this mass mediated consumer culture that a true Chinese popular mass movement, deeply rooted in the public mentality and society, took shape in China for the very first time.[64] The new consumer culture and media created a community by tying together people with a common language and common interests.[65] But something more than CCP-supported patriotism and new commercialized media technologies was necessary to fuel such an intense passion for the nation. The missing piece, I would argue, came in the form of an imagined relationship to the Other.

In the first years of the 1990s, coinciding with the emerging consumer culture, a number of books about Chinese students or immigrant workers in the United States, Europe, and Japan started to appear. The popularity of these books soon exploded generating a new genre of *liuxuesheng wenxue*, émigré literature. Beginning with the wildly popular 1992 *Manhadun zhongguou nuren* (*A Chinese Woman in Manhattan*), uncountable numbers of similar-sounding titles appeared in small outdoor bookstalls across the country. For the first time in the PRC, a book genre had developed in response to commercial mechanisms, driven equally by popular demand and skillful marketing.

In the wake of these works about émigré students, the political literature of "China's New Nationalism" had a similar conception. In 1996 Chinese bookstores were hit by two books, both cleverly marketed and written by Chinese with journalistic, entrepreneurial backgrounds and, most important, living in the United States. In shrill nationalistic language *Zhongguo keyi shuo bu* (*China Can Say No*), soon followed by *Yaomohua Zhongguo de beiho* (*The Plot to Demonize China*), both accused Western powers of wanting to stop China from retaking its rightful place on the world stage. The Chinese coauthors of *Yaomohua Zhongguo* had experienced life in the United States and were familiar with both the Western media profession and American academia. *Zhongguo keyi shuo bu* was soon made into a series on national television, just as Cao Guilin's book *Beijingren zai niuyue* (*A Beijing Man in New York*) became the basis of a soap opera made by the master of the popular and provocative, Wang Shuo.[66]

The demand for this genre of nationalistic populist diatribes against China's perceived Other was insatiable. Just as with the immigrant literature, a large number of books, television programs, and articles followed. These nationalist works, like the émigré literature, appeared in a new cultural setting of consumption and market demand. *China Can Say No* sold 50,000 copies in just a few days, *A Chinese Woman in Manhattan* 500,000 in its first year alone.[67]

Both of these two genres, popular nationalism and émigré literature, focused in on China's relations with the Western Other. While the nationalist texts brimmed with a belief in the imminent power of China to escape the shackles of the containing Other, the émigré literature presented success stories of Chinese individuals succeeding in the West. As film and literature critic Dai Jinhua—who argues that these stories created a new "China-centric imaginary"—remarked, they could be quite chauvinistic in depicting personal triumph as victories of China, while also portraying Chinese as hard-working and superior to other races.[68] Nevertheless, she cautions, there is at the same time inscribed in these stories a stereotype of the "racial superiority of blond, blue-eyed people."[69]

THE NEED FOR RECOGNITION

With China reentering a Western-centered world order, Hegel's argument about the absolute demand for *recognition* turns out to be critical for understanding the emotional dynamics behind the wave of Chinese nationalism.[70] Similar to the émigré genre, populist nationalist literature also obsesses with the Chinese relation to the Other and China's success or failure internationally. However, the tone is rawer here and the revenge meted out is for real. In this nationalist literature, the West is accused of hindering Chinese attempts to progress and from becoming rich and glorious. Similar ideas at the personal level, of course, appear in the émigré genre when a Chinese protagonist encounters the very real racism directed against Asians in the West. However, the emigrants transcend this challenge by succeeding personally and ascending socially. *Zhongguo keyi shuo bu* and similar nationalist texts, on the other hand, protest against an unfair world order and call for the use of political and military power to dismantle this very order.

Influential social thinkers like Benedict Anderson or Ernest Gellner interpret nationalism as both constructed by its usefulness for certain groups of actors and as an almost automatic effect of technical, cultural, and politico-economic changes in modern industrial societies. In his article "Deconstructing the Chinese Nation," historian Prasenjit Duara argues against such standard perceptions of nationalism. For Duara, nationalism is not to be reduced to a construct or invention of modernity. As a China scholar, he is clearly influenced by American historian Joseph Levenson's theory on the particularity of China. Being a civilization and not just a nation, China is the exception and, following Levenson, can therefore be said to have possessed a national identity well before the West's arrival on the scene. Duara does redress a weakness in Levenson's argument—that nationalism was just reflecting the privileged bureaucracy's loyalty to the dynasty they served. Proceeding from the notion of the Other, Duara instead argues that the reason nationalism always existed in China was the various threats presented by external forces, for instance, the Manchu, the Mongols, and the West. It is these Others that prompt the construction of a Chinese identity akin to that of modern nationalism. In this interpretation, nationalism is *relational*, not born out of self-realization or imagined communities. National identity turns into a question of a changing interplay between Self and Other and just as in Hegel's dialectics of recognition, the nation become a nation only after it is recognized as such by an Other.[71]

In her study of immigrant literature, Dai Jinhua posits that the roots of this genre lay in realizations the Chinese made during the 1980s about lack of recognition by the Western Other.[72] In this transitional decade, after being isolated from the rest of the world for so long, Chinese students and others were again able to travel to the West. Their sudden discovery that China was not the center of the universe made the reencounter "deeply shocking and traumatic," Dai argues. The Chinese students realized that Westerners did not expect or even wish a coming world revolution led by China, which was regarded as just another underdeveloped nation.[73] That revelation, as Dai Jinhua argues, produced a "deep sense of anxiety about a national identity in crisis" in the 1980s.[74]

Zhang Xudong suggests that it was this traumatic realization of China's insignificance in the eyes of the West, together with commercialized media and culture, that fueled the new Chinese nationalism of the mid-1990s.[75] "When the post-revolutionary masses encountered Western images of and discourses on China," a new nationalist sentiment emerged, Zhang argues.[76] In his view, the scrutiny by the foreign Other set in motion those powerful emotional forces that erupted as a "new Chinese nationalism"—a negative reaction to the Other's view of China.

RACIAL CASTRATION

David Eng, a specialist on Asian American literature at Pennsylvania University, has come to the conclusion that the Asian-American experience is dominated by a gender complex he calls "racial castration."[77] Migration is not just so much organized ("managed," in his terminology) by ethnicity or nationality but by a particular sexual matrix. This main argument of his book on Asian-American literature concludes that in Western sexual fantasy, Asian men are feminized to the point that they are bereaved of the main symbol of power and masculinity. Of course this condition is not limited to only one side but plays out in a dialectical manner. Eng takes as one of his more elucidating examples to illustrate this complex concept of racial castration, the play *M. Butterfly.*[78] An intervention in the discussion about race and multiculturalism, Chinese-American David Henry Hwang's play tells about a French diplomat stationed in Beijing during the Cultural Revolution. A fan of European opera (especially Puccini), he frequents Beijing Opera productions and falls in love with, not, we would argue, a Chinese actor, but rather the role he is playing.

The Frenchman has not realized that the beautiful woman he sees on the stage is really a man working as a spy for the Chinese government. Initiating a love relationship that lasts for a full eighteen years, the Chinese man playing a woman even produces a baby to present to the diplomat lover. During all those years the Frenchman believes he has a heterosexual relationship with a Chinese woman. The reason his lover would not disrobe during sex, as he saw it, was that being a *Chinese woman* she was extremely shy. After being apprehended during a trip to Paris, the cross-dressing Chinese agent described to a French court some anatomical machinations with which he made the French lover believe he was engaging in heterosexual intercourse, claiming to have the ability to literally lose his balls by making them retrieve up into his body. That the Frenchman disavows his dream-lover's penis becomes for Professor David Eng a perfect illustration of the lengths to which Westerners in an inverted fetishism are willing to go to make disappear a phallus that in reality is there.[79]

Sigmund Freud termed the flows, obstructions, and tendencies running human interaction *libido*. This pulsating force of psychic energy relates to unconscious desire and demand belonging to the Ego. But as society restricts, desire is suppressed and sublimated, which Freud realized leads to neurotic complications such as hysteria. His early career traced many such cases in which identity and sexual fixation of libido had gone astray in childhood traumas. Freud thus explained his general theory in a semi-mythological family drama of love and rejection, central to which was the threat of castration and (mis)realization around having, lacking, and being the phallus that later in life will structure any individual's flows of desire and his objects of love. In Jacques Lacan's rereading of Freud, this (castrated) phallus takes on a different, symbolic meaning; it now signifies a universal order, propped up by the Law and the Name of the Father while simultaneously throwing a powerful veil over the retroactive trauma caused by absence. In his theory on sexuality and desire, Lacan explains how, in an intricate dialectic centered on this lack, man symbolically *possesses* this phallus, while woman exists in a masquerade of dressing up as *being* the phallus.

We suggest in the following that this logic, of *having* versus *being* it for someone else, organizes a sexual geopolitics of Chinese foreign relations symbolically and can be used to clarify the vicissitudes and libidinal underpinnings of not just contemporary Chinese nationalism but also a global imaginary expressed in popular culture, news media, and political discourse of the transformative 1990s—just when the post-Cold War order was negotiated. *The Libidinal Economy of China* therefore lays out the significance of sexual fantasy and gender in the discourse of national identity and the foreign Other. More specifically it analyzes the relationship between China and the West in the realms of the Real, the Symbolic, and the Imaginary. The following exploration is thus also, on a different level, about the libidinal economy globally, that is, of an imaginary China. In sum, this study sets out to unravel a sexual geopolitics by describing the link popular culture and nationalist discourse often strike between "femininity" and "China." Applying the language of psychoanalysis it attempts to approach the sexual fantasy underpinning Sino-Western relations.

NOTES

1. Foreign Relations of the United States, 1969–1976, Vol. XVIII, China, 1973–1976, Document 1. Memorandum of Conversation1 Beijing, February 17–18,

1973, 11:30 p.m.–1:20 a.m. https://history.state.gov/historicaldocuments/frus1969-76v18/d12.

2. McCracken 1988, 3.

3. Slater 1997, 8.

4. For an introduction to consumer culture, see Featherstone 1991, Slater 1997, or Lury 1996.

5. Featherstone 1987, 17, 18.

6. Campbell 1989.

7. Pollay 1984.

8. Ewen 1976, 19.

9. Ewen and Ewen 1982.

10. Featherstone 1982.

11. Laermas 1993, 82.

12. Quoted from Stross 1993, 255.

13. "Zhongshi shenghuo fangshi de biange" ("Emphasize changes in lifestyles"), *Renmin Ribao* (*People's Daily*), Oct. 12, 1984.

14. Chai 1992, 721.

15. Other lists of consumer products were the "Four Musts" (bicycle, radio, wristwatch, and sewing machine) and later, the "Big Eight" (color TV, refrigerator, stereo equipment, camera, motorbike, suite of furniture, washing machine, and electric fan).

16. Cheng, Allen Tien-jen 1995, 56.

17. *China: Consumer Trends,* 1993, 15.

18. Goodman 1996, 226.

19. McKillop 1993, 25.

20. Todd Crowell and David Hsieh, "Little Emperors: Is China's One Child Policy Creating a Society of Brats," (Asiaweek-December 1, 1995) http://www.pathfinder.com/@@il2xEQUA, refers to a study by James McNeal (Texas A&M University), in which he shows that in China children's preferences influence 69 percent of purchases against only 40 percent in the United States. In 1994, a CCTV report on youth consumption asked children on the streets about their consumption habits. High school children in Beijing were shown to have up to 100 yuan a month to spend, in addition to which they received *hongbao*, or gifts of money, of between 500 yuan and a few thousand yuan every Chinese New Year.

21. See Zhao Bin and Graham Murdock, "Young Pioneers: Children and the Making of Chinese Consumerism," in *Cultural Studies* 10(2) (1996): 215.

22. See for example, Wang Xiong's article, "*Hua! Jingren de xuesheng xiaofeichao*" (*Alarming trends in school children's consumption*) *Caifeng* 2 (1993): 18–24.

23. However, as Deborah Davies and Julia Sensenbrenner (2000) show in an interesting study, the money spent on the single child can also be understood symbolically and therefore be as much about the parents and grandparents desire to foot the bill.

24. See Wang Jing 2008, 26.

25. Belk 1988, 103. Even if there is reason for caution about embracing a perception of a "normal" or First World consumption pattern, the enormous contrast between poverty on the one hand and conspicuous consumption in large cities of the developing world on the other clearly supports the idea of a Third World consumerism.

26. Huang Ping 1995.

27. All this was, of course, still an urban phenomenon in the 1990s. For a good collection of studies on various aspects of urban consumption in China, see Davies 2000.

28. Huang Ping 1995.

29. In 1946 there were around 100 advertising agencies in China (see Rice and Zaiming 1988, 43, 44).

30. Ding Yunpeng, 1979.

31. Ibid.

32. Kong and Laurence 1993, 181.

33. Stross 1990, 486.

34. Kong and Laurence 1993, 181.

35. The industry was soon organized as a government-led network with the China National Advertising Corporation at the top, and a series of local agencies like the Beijing Advertising Corporation and the Shanghai Advertising and Decoration Corporation under it. But since TV stations, magazines, and newspapers had their own creative staff, many ads were produced outside of the official agency structure.

36. Wang Jian 1998.

37. Chadwick 1997, 285.

38. For a more thorough account of the discussion about the legitimization of advertising in China in the 1980s, see Wacker 1991, 180–235.

39. Stross 1990, 487.

40. Ibid., 496. As anti-Japanese sentiments resurfaced in 1986, it was especially Japanese advertising that was attacked as when Beijing authorities issued a ban on outdoor billboard advertising and removed several Japanese billboards from Chang'an Avenue (see Reaves 1986, 9).

41. Stross 1993, 237.

42. Ibid., 242. Even more sensitive was when politicians appeared in ads, which led to immediate reactions, for example, when an ad for Maotai liquor featured President Jiang Zemin.

43. Ogilvy & Mather's regional director in Hong Kong, Harry Reid, quoted in Lynne Reaves, "China: A New Frontier for Advertisers," *Advertising Age*, September 16, 1985, 74.

44. Stewart and Campbell 1988.

45. Marketing surveys revealed that people enjoyed watching commercials on television. In a 1987 report, for example, 96 percent of a sample of Beijing residents said they enjoyed watching television commercials for any consumer product (Stross 1993, 239). A visiting scholar from the Chinese Academy of Social Sciences researcher frankly asked me, "When there is no advertising on TV, how do Swedes know what to buy?"

46. In 1994, marketing research company D'Arcy, Marcius, Benton & Bowles published a report showing that Chinese to a higher degree than consumers in other countries relied on advertising to make up their minds on the quality and value of different products and brands.

47. Although it was taken for granted by Western commentators that American products would be advertised and craved, the truth was that in the first part of the

1980s, it was mainly Japanese electronics companies running ads in Chinese newspapers, on billboards, and on television. Not until the mid-1980s was there much foreign advertising in Chinese media, and virtually all such advertising was done by the Japanese (Stewart and Campbell 1988, 318). Furthermore, while the Japanese advertising agency Dentsu was quick to set up office inside China, most American agencies operated out of their offices in Hong Kong. Japanese companies not only used advertising to promote themselves, they also engaged in public relations, sponsorship, and other goodwill activities. They promoted sporting activities like the Beijing Marathon as well as various music galas, and saw to it that they were broadcast on Chinese national television.

48. "Madison Avenue in China," *San Francisco Chronicle,* March 25, 1979.

49. Shanghai Advertising Corporation ran an ad on the last page of the *Beijing Review* in March 1979, offering foreign businesses help with advertising.

50. Stross 1990, 493. *Hongqi* had one restriction: they did not accept ads for Coca-Cola.

51. Wang Shaoguang 1995, 159. For a sociological description of television in China during the 1980s, see Lull 1991.

52. Karp 1994, 47.

53. In 1982 CCTV was given 60 hours of American programs. In return CCTV had to broadcast 320 minutes of advertising for IBM, Boeing, Procter & Gamble, Kodak, and a number of other U.S.-based multinational corporations. In another deal CCTV was allowed to select 52 feature films from Twentieth Century Fox. In exchange for advertising time CCTV got another 100 hours of MCA/Paramount/MGM (Lull 1991, 149).

54. Yu Huang 1994, 227.

55. Interview in May 1994 at the Advertising Department (Guanggaosi) of the National Bureau for the Management and Administration of Industry and Commerce (Guojia gong shang xingzheng guanliju).

56. When Australian media mogul Robert Murdoch bought Star TV in 1993 and declared information technology a threat to totalitarian regimes all over the world, the Chinese government responded by banning the purchase and use of satellite dishes. Murdoch repented by withdrawing the BBC news channel from the satellite (Karp1994, 48, and Karp 1993, 72).

57. The most brazen display of the commercialization of media appeared as some journalists started selling their services to anyone willing to pay for a story. They took bribes for writing positively about companies and reportedly blackmailed officials and State corporations by threatening to write critical reports (Karp 1993). "Young reporters are cheaper than advertising and more effective," was how a Beijing newspaper editor explained it. Commercialism thus blurred the distinction between advertising and journalism just as effectively as politics had up to that point blurred the distinction between propaganda and news.

58. Ibid.

59. Hong Junhao 1994.

60. See Anderson 1983.

61. "My beloved Party, my loving mother, I am always your loving son," as the propaganda character Lei Feng liked to end his diary entries.

62. For the following see Viroli 1997, 63-65.
63. For this and the following, see Zheng Wang 2013, 95–117.
64. Zhang 2008, 109.
65. Zhang 1998, 114.
66. That soap opera was shot at great expense on location in New York and aired in 1993.
67. Zhang 2008, 186.
68. Dai 2002, 196.
69. Ibid., 197.
70. Most political and social theory about recognition proceeds from Hegel's ideas on the master-slave dialectic. German sociologist Axel Honneth instead returns to the earlier Hegel and a discussion on the importance of the Other for creating the Self. Honneth takes this a step further and looks at self-recognition and anxiety via Freud and Donald Winnicot. His argument is that anxiety arises from a baby's fear of being left alone by its love object, its mother. This implies an existential and universal basis for a theory of recognition.
71. See Prasenjit Duara's 1993 article. The PRC had been kept outside for so long, not accepted universally, and held in isolation also by its own leaders.
72. Dai 2002, 192.
73. Ibid.
74. Ibid.
75. First in Zhang Xudong's 1998 article and then also in his 2008 book.
76. See Zhang Xudong 2008, 109.
77. Eng 2001.
78. Hugely popular and polemic, this theater production was later turned into a film by acclaimed director David Cronenberg. As effective as the play itself, the film captures the complicated postcolonial politics between China and the West, while also unintentionally reinforcing a Chinese victimization discourse. All of this is clad in a story on gender transgression, female masquerade, love, and sex. For the true story behind the play, see Wadler 1993.
79. Instead of, as in Freudian fetishism, seeing a penis where there is none, they do not see a penis where there is one.

Chapter One

Femininity after Mao

Woman in Advertising and Consumer Culture

We described above the birth of Western consumer culture and, arguably, also of modern life where identity is no longer ascribed or anchored in tradition or religion but something that individuals create for themselves and where marketing feeds on the resulting crisis of identity by associating commodities with feelings, emotions, and lifestyles. Modern consumer culture, in this respect, is reflexive, if not narcissistic—occupied with self-image through various projects of creating and transforming personalities, styles, and looks.[1] Sociologists like Chris Shilling and Anthony Giddens thus argue that identity in late capitalism turned into a body project.[2] In consumer culture the way we look to others comes to rule how we perceive ourselves, and advertising was momentous in bringing forward this "new Self" of beauty and masquerade.

The development of consumer culture in the West was a catalyst also for women's liberation. Shopping malls were the first public space where middle-class women could go and meet other women without a male escort.[3] It has further been suggested that women were not just the primary object of consumption, but that consumer culture itself was in the throes of feminization. Not only is contemporary femininity a construct of consumer culture, but this consumer culture is, in fact, a result of femininity itself. As sociologist Celia Lury puts it:

> This line of argument makes a case for a view of women as active intermediaries in the development of consumer culture, indicating how a specifically feminine subjectivity provides the basis for the emergence of an aestheticized mode of using objects and creating one's own identity. From this point of view, the gendered process of objectification and the associated relations of looking are not only a consequence of consumer culture, but also a causal factor in its development.[4]

The "gendered process of objectification and the associated relations of looking" refer, of course, to what has been described as "the male gaze" and the fact that in advertising women take the place of the objects they are selling. Judith Williamson in her study on the semiotics of advertising explains how this magic worked. Using an ad for Chanel perfume with a close-up of Catherine Deneuve's face and the words "Chanel No. 5," Williamson points out that, despite the fact that nothing in the ad explicitly states it, most of us would draw the conclusion that this particular perfume is for chic, beautiful, and glamorous people.[5] Using the metaphor of trade, a transfer of value takes place from Catherine Deneuve to the perfume bottle.[6] But it is not Catherine Deneuve herself that gives value to the bottle; it is what her image means to us. According to this analysis advertising fetishizes commodities. By the use of a beautiful *woman,* signification is transferred from one sign system—that of famous people—to another sign system—that of perfumes. And in this example, advertising first constructs women as objects of desire and then refers to and transfers this appeal to pretty much anything it wants to.[7]

Williamson is careful to point out that ads mean something only to someone, that the receiver is the creator of meaning. Ads offer meaning to us, and we give meaning to them.[8] Borrowing from Jacques Lacan, she describes how ads appeal to us because they present us with a coherent, unified Self, something all of us desire but can never attain. What the advertisement does is represent the object of desire, which is, in fact, the "Self." This function of ads—to represent to us an image of a coherent, unified Self—is, she says, the ruse that drives much of the ad business.

Advertising thus resembles Lacan's "mirror phase," metaphorically expressing the identity-construction process by which the subject constantly mirrors itself in the seemingly more perfect others. The self-awareness of a baby consists at first of a diffuse unity with the surrounding world—a primary realm of sameness that Lacan calls the Imaginary.[9] At about six months, the child encounters her image in a mirror, recognizes that it is really she, but at the same time perceives this unity as an "Other," as someone different from herself. The mirror, which is perceived as an Other person, has a unity that the observing child lacks. This "imaged-I" of the mirror reflection becomes an "Ideal-Ego" that expresses the desire to exist in a situation where subject and object are not yet separated. This desire remains with the child after entering what Lacan calls the Symbolic order: the preexisting structures into which the child is eventually socialized.[10] According to Lacan, we all strive for this "Ideal-Ego" but since it is only attainable in the Imaginary, we never fulfill our desire to become this coherent, unified Self. As Williamson points out, this is also how advertisements work. They offer us an image of ourselves that we can aspire to but never achieve. Every individual interaction with an advertisement that presents an image of another person represents the step in Lacan's identity creation that constitutes a fictional creation of a unified Self.

If we proceed from how "woman" in advertising functions as a *signifier*, what then is her meaning in the libidinal economy of our own times? Sigmund Freud held that men *have*, but women *are*, the phallus. Being the phallus is, in this logic, not a privileged position since it entails being it for someone else. Such a Freudian interpretation holds women as objects to be exchanged. Historically and in various cultural settings, women also served as gifts presented between men, exemplified, for example, by the intricate relationship between the royal houses of Europe, the widespread custom of the bride replacing her family name with that of her husband, or the way some cultures regard daughters as less valuable because they will be wedded off to another family.[11]

The women trafficked in this way between men and families do not possess an identity, the argument goes, but instead reflect masculine identity.[12] We have here a similarity with and an understanding of the role of women in consumer culture. If in premodern kinship systems woman functioned as a gift circulated between families, clans, or villages, bringing about and constructing identity, social position, recognition, and relations between groups, then in capitalism her importance symbolically stands in direct opposition to her decreased reproductional importance. Ours is thus a cultural economy manufacturing the belief in satisfying a desire that builds on the very void that advertising covers up with seductive images of women, i.e., images promising a full identity through the consumption of goods.

THE BEAUTY OF WOMAN

The logic is thus established that images of beautiful women transfer social value to objects. If at the same time the purpose of women is to establish bonds between male communities or families, then it is this quality that woman takes on in consumer culture. If in premodern societies young brides were trafficked as objects between men to establish social relations, in modern consumer culture beautiful women are used to transfer imaginary social value to commodities whose consumption provides us with social meaning as we invent parts of our identities phantasmatically. Once again the exchange of women constitutes identity. We should neither be surprised by nor take for granted the fact that the post-Mao era in China, together with the advent of a consumer culture, saw a return not of *gender*, as is often stated, but more precisely of *femininity*. But in an international order this sexual logic, as we saw in David Eng, gets tangled up with geopolitics, power, and wealth.

China was once the center of the world and had no need for foreign ideas or technologies. Instead, foreign states flocked to the Middle Kingdom to trade and present tribute, reassuring the Chinese emperor that he was ruling *Tianxia* (*all under heaven*). Then came the British ironclad gunboats and enforced a treaty system on China. The defeat at the hands of the Japanese in 1894 intensified a sense of crisis. The anxiety that China was now going to be "cut up like a melon" channeled a great deal of energy into the vision of the Chinese woman as a weak victim.[13] The thinking, advanced by the two most important protagonists in the early creation of modern Chinese nationalism, Kang Youwei and his disciple, Liang Qichao, focused on the idea that Chinese women were suppressed by the patriarchy of an old Confucian social order. For them, China risked being fully conquered by the West because the Chinese patriarchy had weakened its women by practices such as foot binding and binding of breasts. This critical view of a thousand-year-old cultural tradition led Kang Youwei to petition the emperor to abolish foot binding. While these early efforts to reform China were crushed, a sense of crisis intensified, accompanied by a realization of the role of the female body in overcoming the threat of foreign imperialism. As Yang Mayfair succinctly put it, "The liberation of women was always tied in with the liberation of the nation, so that the former was a means to an end of the latter struggle."[14] The May 4th Movement transformed the question of the suppression of women into a radical critique of China's civilization. Confucianism was said to oppose modernity, and women had to be liberated from Confucian patriarchy in a manner that mirrored how the nation's survival hinged on being liberated from imperialism.

The Communists shared this attention to the female body and its beautification. When a young Mao Zedong—clearly influenced by Engels's description of woman as the slave of man—formulated his views on gender differences and feminine adornment, he did it in penal terms, arguing:

> If a woman's head and a man's head are actually the same, and there is no real difference between a woman's waist and a man's, why must women have their hair piled up in those ostentatious and awkward buns? Why must they wear those messy skirts cinched tightly at the waist? I think women are regarded as criminals to start with, and tall buns and long skirts are the instruments of torture applied to them by men. There is also their facial make-up, which is the brand of a criminal; the jewelry on their hands, which constitutes shackles; and their pierced ears and bound feet, which represent corporal punishment.[15]

In the particular libidinal economy China's Communist Party introduced, desire was displaced onto the Party and the task of revolution. Both men and women were now encouraged to wear a male uniform said to represent workers, farmers, and soldiers—the heroes of the Revolution. These two-piece outfits were either dark blue or gray trousers and jacket, or the green Army outfit so popular in the 1960s and '70s. Sartorial uniformity was however only a first step in effectively annulling the social capital of femininity. During the Cultural Revolution the only hairstyle permitted for women of marriageable age was the short bob-cut; Red Guards roamed the streets and forcibly cut off women's braids.[16] Any attention paid by women to fashion, beauty, and adornment was considered bourgeois, counterrevolutionary, or simply criminal. A well-known case of this sexual regime was the public humiliation of President Liu Shaoqi's wife, Wang Guangmei, for wearing a patterned *qipao* dress in public during a State visit to Indonesia[17]—her offense being that she, as a representative of China, had presented herself as a woman.

As we understand from the quote above, Mao did not differentiate between women's and men's bodies. To increase the workforce, China's Communist Party put forward new role models for women as the heroic, hard-working "Iron Girl Brigades." Both Chinese and foreign commentators at the time saw this disavowal of femininity as something positive—part of a successful feminist attempt to eradicate the inequalities between men and women. In hindsight, however, the Communist Revolution did not lead to true equality between women and men that many imagined. Instead, as Elisabeth Croll puts it, "The Chinese women were only living the revolutionary rhetoric."[18] In reality women often were expected not only to do the same work as men but also run the household. The childcare, cleaning, and cooking, however, were made invisible. With the new marriage law implemented soon after liberation, a truly radical push for gender equality was set in motion, but the Communist leadership clearly regarded women also as a vast labor reserve in the service of the Revolution. Women's bodies were disciplined to be *productive* in the sense of serving the State and the economy, while the imaginary register of the *reproductive* economy that would create social bonds was displaced.[19] Literary critic Meng Yue, in her psychoanalytical reading of Chinese revolutionary literature, points out how women in the Mao era were made to sacrifice individuality and femininity for collective interests. Private, personal happiness was reduced to an indirect consequence of the new socialist society. The political code substituted for the sexual in what Meng Yue, paraphrasing Jacques Lacan, calls a "party-centric" symbolic order in which female desire was displaced in favor of the responsibility of carrying out the revolution.[20]

Symbolically though, femininity still played an important (albeit negative) role as female dress and adornment were viewed as signs of individualism; women who paid attention to their appearance and looks were accused of being selfish individualists. "Feminine pleasures and feminine beauty were thus used as a metaphor for moral degeneration or ideological impurity," as sociologist Harriet Evans puts it.[21] In her feminist interpretation, insistence on androgynous dress and the suspicion of any "feminine taste" were related to wishing to control women's desires. The purpose of this control was "to reinforce a representation of sexual order that depended on the woman's denial of potential interests of her own in favor of those defined by external agencies."[22] In such biopolitics, women's desires were reined in and channeled into labor and childbirth.[23]

WOMEN AS CAPITAL

With the economic reforms of Deng Xiaoping moving forward after Mao Zedong's death, beauty could again function as sexual capital.[24] Young, good-looking Chinese women were therefore increasingly employed in selling products, brands, and services in the developing beauty industry. In urban shopping areas passersby were greeted by young, pretty "Miss Welcomes," who invited people to visit the shops. Inside the stores "Miss Shopping Guides" *(daogou xiaojie)* and other young women working behind the counters attended customers. Similarly, pretty women in enticing outfits attracted passersby into restaurants and karaoke bars. Images of good-looking young women smiled out from TV commercials, magazine ads, and huge outdoor billboards. Female beauty, formerly degraded, now, with its erotic appeal, became a valuable asset that could be converted into money.

Not surprisingly, this would create a sharp division between two conflicting value systems. An older generation had grown up during the Revolution and found adaptation to all these changes difficult. For young women, however, the masquerade of femininity quickly became a norm as consumer culture spread its seditious wings into every small nook and cranny of the Empire. We can sense the depth of this generational gap by reading the following two short autobiographical stories from two generations of Chinese women; the first is written by a middle-aged woman who grew up during the Cultural Revolution.[25]

The First Time I Used Make-Up Was in Japan

> Maybe it had to do with my line of work or perhaps it was about the era my generation grew up in, but like many other middle-aged technicians, I had never been willing to spend either money or time on make-up. I had therefore never experienced the enchanting sense of beauty that comes from using cosmetics.
>
> Not long ago I visited Japan as a member of a delegation from our factory. Strolling around in the city I noticed how all the Japanese women, regardless of age and occupation, had put on make-up before going out. This added greatly to their feminine charm and attraction [*shi nüxingde fengyun geng jiadong ren*].

Our Japanese interpreter, Miss Lin, was a very cordial and vivacious young woman. After only a few days together we had already become very familiar. Once when chatting, I let her know that never in my life had I tried make-up. Clearly much surprised on hearing this, she offered to help me to apply some.

I declined politely but our factory director, who loved to raise some noise, used the "method of prodding someone into action," saying, "If Miss Lin agrees to help you make yourself up, the whole group supports you."

After this Miss Lin became even more determined. She went down to the hotel shop and, using her own money, bought me a set of cosmetics. Since it would have been most ungracious to not accept such kindness, I suddenly found myself, a stranger in a foreign country, about to be given my first-ever makeover.

Although Miss Lin's skills were nothing out of the ordinary, she managed in just a few moves to make my face look radiant. Powder and mascara erased the wrinkles of age, and my cheeks were painted slightly red. Feelings first of embarrassment, then of excitement came while looking in the mirror at the stranger who was me. This was certainly the way for women to express their innermost craving for beauty and self-esteem!

When she was done, everyone found the result very good, claiming I suddenly looked ten years younger. Amidst the well-meant laughter and voices of approval, Miss Lin stood with a satisfied smile on her face, as if she had just completed a masterpiece. This incident became an amusing memory of our visit to Japan, a memory shared by the whole group.

After we returned home to China, I went back to being the same old me, always rushing between work and family. I haven't had the opportunity to adorn myself since then but often recall the warm scene when, for the first and only time in my life, I was wearing make-up. I don't know if the sweetness of the memory comes from the beauty I was given or of the warm friendship—perhaps a little of both.[26]

Growing up in a time when female beautification had been subjugated to the militant demands of the Revolution and pride in personal appearance was viewed suspiciously, this middle-aged woman had learned to disapprove of female "vanity." Her generation, as she explains, had never used makeup, and even in a foreign capitalist country she needed the approval of her group and its leader before daring to try it. She found Japanese women attractive and beautiful, and was filled with warmth and pleasure when she looked at her own enhanced face in the mirror. However, she also felt that the image she saw was not the real her, that it was just a masquerade. When she returned to China, she reverted to her old ways, busily taking care of others at work and at home.

A young woman in Shanghai has a wholly dissimilar experience. Her account reveals not only a completely different attitude toward cosmetics, women's beauty, and feminine masquerade, but also a relationship to commodities typical of consumer society.

A Red Lipstick

I accompanied A Ning to the store to buy some shampoo. While she was carefully studying the brands and prices of different shampoos, I stuck my hand in my pocket and fingered the scholarship money I had just received. Excited, my gaze wandered off to the left side of the counter—the cosmetics counter—and a red lipstick that was so enticing that I couldn't resist staring. A Ning pulled at me, asking which shampoo was the best. "Piaorou," I answered absentmindedly. While A Ning went to the cashier to pay, I waited for her at the counter. My legs, however, started pulling me toward the left and, behind the display window, the silent line of different colors. The red one made me drool the same way any normal person would in front of a bowl of fresh strawberries. I stared at it with round eyes while a faint smile appeared at the corner of my mouth.

A Ning put the Piaorou shampoo in the bag and looked at me. My attention was still fixed on the cosmetics display window and, as if reading my mind, she said: "Buy one. That red color looks really nice."

"No, I'm not going to buy it. Let's go!" I replied.

After we got back to our dormitory, A Ning poured out some hot water, preparing to try out her shampoo. I stared blankly at the beds.

I keep a little mirror under my pillow. I don't know how it started, but when there's no one around I like to steal a look at myself in that mirror, just to see if I'm pretty or not. The first time I did this, I discovered a tiny black mole on my lower lip. A Ning told me it was a "gluttony mark" and that I could cover it over with some lipstick. In that way I would also be relieved of my big appetite. That a lipstick could cure my big appetite was, of course, a joke, but my small mole had really turned into a serious worry.

From that time on, lipsticks started appearing frequently in my dreams. Sometimes just a single one, sometimes a whole box of them. In my dreams I carefully unscrewed a lipstick, enjoyed its nice fragrance, and then carefully placed it against my lips. . . .

A nice aroma filled the air in our room after A Ning had washed her hair. While combing it out, she said, "It feels good but it was a bit expensive."

"Not that expensive. Compared to the lipstick, it was cheap," I replied.

I opened the cupboard and looked at my wallet. In it I had the pocket money that my father and mother had given me. Together with the scholarship money I had just collected, it was enough for that seductive red lipstick. But then there were also all those books I needed to buy.[27]

From the differing takes on female beauty, the Self, and the use of cosmetics expressed in these two stories, we can sense some of the abrupt changes consumer culture during the 1990s brought to the libidinal economy. The main difference lies in how the two women negotiate social and individual pleasures, and responsibilities. While the older woman does not let her desire for looking good get in the way of her social duties, the young woman seems totally consumed by a vain and narcissistic desire. Both stories touch upon friendship and grooming. While the older woman experienced a close and warm friendship with the Japanese interpreter, the younger one is so obsessed with the lipstick that she becomes unconscious of her friend. Her attention wavers between worries about her looks and the seductive commodity. Drawn to the counter with the red lipstick, she is oblivious to the rest of the world.[28]

For the young woman in the letter recounted above, beauty and the power to seduce and charm was no longer anything to be ashamed of. Rather it had, although contested, become the hegemonic ideal. The psychological patterns of the young woman resemble descriptions of narcissism in Western consumer culture.[29] Where premodern China was a patriarchy and where individual desire and pleasure were channeled into collective efforts during the Mao era, the 1990s introduced commodity fetishism together with a narcissistic obsession with the Self. While Maoist gender politics strove to displace heterosexually directed desire onto the Revolution, the nation, and the Party by breaking up the family and condemning female beauty as criminal individualism, under the influences of a modern consumer culture feminine pleasure in beautification now takes on exactly the extreme forms of individualism it had previously been accused of, but now with society's approval.[30] A flagrant example was the return of beauty contests.

Under Mao it was argued beauty contests had served as a way for nationalist party leaders to find mistresses, but in the 1990s they were all the rage again. Women competed to become, for example, *Liyi xiaojie* (Miss Manners) of Beijing, *Rongcheng xiaojie* (Miss Chengdu), and *Yueji xiaojie* (Miss Rose) of Tianjin.[31] Other contests took different forms. When the Asian Games were held in Beijing in 1990, a competition for Miss Foreign Company Advertising Model saw 2,000 models, each representing a certain company and product, compete.[32] In the widely covered Chinese Air Hostesses Beauty Contest, women were not only employed to sell a certain product but—plausibly inspired by the campaigns of various East Asian airlines—the women-as-(air) hostesses were part of the very product they sold.[33] There were also Miss Advertisement and Miss Chinese Advertisement Model contests in which professional advertising models competed with each other. In these contests, the winners' good looks were sometimes rewarded not just with prize money, but also with employment. Some women from the countryside even won urban residence permits through these contests.[34]

As it was now common practice to employ young women in various occupations solely based on their good looks, female beauty was becoming a commodity in and of itself. Many young women thus found work as a *bailing xiaojie* (white-collar misses) either as secretaries or in public relations departments, while others were employed as advertising and fashion models or guides.[35] Their function was to be pleasant decoration, offering assistance when business partners visited a company or joining their bosses on business trips. These white-collar misses were required to be young and good-looking, and to know how to flaunt those qualities.

The social transformation described above did not take place, of course, without active intervention from the Party apparatus. Already before "liberation"in its base area around Yanan, CCP set up a women's organization to function as a united front organization. After 1959 it became known as the All-China Women's Federation (with the Chinese acronym *Fulian).* Although acting a little more independent during the 1990s, it was still by function a Communist Party organization whose task was to tie Chinese women to the Party-State policy. In a series of articles the official women's magazine, *Zhongguo funü*—run by Fulian—invited readers to discuss the feminine practice of "eating from the rice bowl of youth." Despite the fact that the editors themselves talked about the dangers of "youthism" (*qingchunzhuyi*), "money worship" (*baijinzhuyi*), and "hedonism" (*xianglezhuyi*), the majority of letters published expressed sympathy for women who used their youthful good looks to earn a living.[36] Since these letters and editorials give an insight not only into how women in China viewed this matter but also reveal the position of the All-China Women's Federation's, let us briefly look at their content.

One letter is from an eighteen-year-old high school student whose parents were doing everything in their power to get her to a university.[37] When she was younger, the girl did not mind her parents forcing her to study hard; however, one day she asked to take singing lessons and her parents said no, refusing even to buy her a karaoke set so she could practice at home. The 18-year-old after this could no longer see the point of studying—science was boring, the humanities would only make her poor, and the competition for getting into foreign business schools was too hard. She believed that in order to get married, she had to be good-looking. And as good looks now could be purchased, she needed money. Maybe she would be better off working in a restaurant or beauty parlor than attending a university. A friend of hers was a server in a restaurant at the Olympic Village in Beijing. With all the tips she got from foreign guests and businessmen, she was able to buy 400-*yuan* Italian shoulder bags and luxurious 80-*yuan* lipsticks. This girlfriend of hers also had a lot of men who took her out dancing or to the movies. Our young eighteen-year-old was clearly envious of the money and attention her friend was receiving and had decided to not follow her parents' wishes. She believed she could easily find a job since she was under twenty, tall, and quite good-looking. Her plan was to earn some money and then study at a beauty school, an education that might make it possible for her to support herself while she tried to become a singer.

The readers of *Zhongguo funü* in their contributions to the magazines often discussed which was best for young women: to "eat from the ricebowl of youth" *(chi qingchun fan)* or to attend college.[38] Those who argued for the former seemed enthralled by the opportunity to buy fashionable clothes, shoes, and cosmetics. In one letter a student of literature said she was shocked when a classmate dropped out of university to start working as a "public relations girl."[39] Later, however, the classmate dressed in beautiful clothes, had a fashionable haircut, wore perfume, and carried a beeper. Bitter at being a poor student unable even to buy her own schoolbooks, she asked why good looks had suddenly become so important. Although our student understood that the kind of job her former classmate now had—entertaining older businessmen with female charm and youthful beauty—was not very glamorous, she nevertheless questioned her own prudent lifestyle.

Although some letters expressed the conventional wisdom that good employment and lifestyle would be achieved through studies, not good looks, most readers agreed that feminine beauty was a valuable asset that could lead to employment and a good salary. One letter not only expressed unreserved approval of the contemporary focus on feminine beauty, it also voiced sharp criticism of the ideals and realities that women had encountered previously, under Mao Zedong's regime:

> They are changing. Their clothes are getting more fashionable, their jewelry increasingly expensive, and their make-up more high-class. But most important, they are providing more and more to society, and society gets increasingly dependent upon them. The contemporary images of women are full of vitality, self-esteem, and charming faces. They are successively replacing the pale, sick-looking faces of yesterday's women, surrounded as they were by kitchen utensils, men, and children. This replacement is about the new substituting the old. It is the progress of society, an expression of civilization, and the embodiment of our value as women.[40]

As we have seen, the All-China Women's Federation—the Communist Party organization in charge of gender politics—promoted in its premier mouthpiece, *Zhongguo funü*, a femininity predicated on beauty, fashion, and good makeup skills. This particular femininity was depicted as liberating, setting women free of the "kitchen prison" and letting them live a life of their own, full of vitality and self-esteem.

In reality as the economy tsar, Zhu Rongji, was discussing dismantling the State sector of the economy—threatening to create mass layoffs and social unrest—many women were already experiencing something of a backlash. Young women who would be disproportionally hit by layoffs were being advised to embrace professions that had them actually selling their beauty to men.

STATE CONSUMERISM

Precious little was written in the 1990s by scholars in China or abroad about this movement toward modern consumer culture turning beauty into a valuable asset. Australian sociologist Beverly Hooper, however, made some observations on the relationship between consumerism, women, and the State.[41] Her assessment was that the unfolding of a consumer culture in relation to women was following the pattern of other societies. Chinese women were drawn into the "logic of global consumer culture" and made objects for consumption, just as had happened to their Western sisters. The big difference, of course, was that for Chinese women, this development occurred in a country with a Communist leadership promoting socialist values. Looking at the new images of women in the commercial press and advertising, Hooper concluded that Chinese consumer culture reinforced domestic roles for women together as well as a commoditization and objectification of the female body. Consumer culture thus reinforced the "double burden" (work and housework) that Chinese women have struggled with at least since the founding of the People's Republic. Quoting Chinese columnist Cai Hong, Hooper claimed that advertising "legitimizes the stereotyped roles of women as temptress, wife, and mother."[42] While such viewpoints could have been delivered by any feminist, even with little or no familiarity with the Chinese context, Hooper's most important insight is her suggestion that the gender construction of consumer culture was reinforced by the Chinese State. The Communist leadership that formerly denounced the commercial exploitation of women through the voice of the All-China Women's Federation now was pushing such constructions of femininity.[43]

Sinologist Harriet Evans took a position similar to that of Hooper. Evans describes the implications this new consumer culture has for women as "the predictable consequence of the permeation of patriarchal structures by commercial values widely associated with the material culture of the West."[44] Evans acknowledges that there existed a legitimate right to individual self-expression outside collective responsibilities together with an opportunity to test new understandings of femininity produced by fashion. But she then harked back to a traditional feminist critique of fashion, saying that when feminine beauty serves to satisfy others, it "subordinates pleasure in sartorial experimentation to the final approval of the male other."[45] Evans, however, also makes another important comment on Western beauty imagery in Chinese fashion magazines and advertising, writing, "The West is simultaneously constructed as an object of desire and . . . a source of danger, contamination, and disease."[46]

This critique of the role of the West in the bourgeoning consumer culture of the 1990s was nothing new, and for China it did not originate in any feminist or Communist perspective. Already in the 1930s there was widespread anxiety and debate over the so-called "New" or "Modern" woman and the role of foreign merchandise and manners. In his seminal study on consumption and nationalism in 1930s China, Karl Gerth devotes a chapter to how the consumer practices of urban women were believed to threaten China.[47] *Modern* was at the time often conflated with *Western*, and for the patriotic consumption movement the modern woman was especially threatening; it was after all women who made most consumer choices and who educated a new generation of consumers. Now this modern woman, a consuming creature who did nothing productive and was defined by her outgoing attitudes and activities, threatened to ruin China with her weakness for foreign fashion and cosmetics. China was on the verge of destruction, it was said, because these women could not control their impulses.

In the following chapters we will discuss in detail Chinese femininity and beauty ideals in advertising and women's magazines during the 1990s, track the role of the Party in reformulating femininity, and relate this libidinal economy with consumer culture and society at large to see how it deals with the desire for and fear of the West referred to by Harriet Evans above.

NOTES

1. For more about the Self in consumer culture, see Slater 1997, 83–97.
2. See Shilling 2013 and Giddens 1991. See also Bryan Turner's (1996) discussion of the project of the Self in the late modern age.
3. Laermas 1993, 86–89. All this happened in Paris and London around the same time as the emergence of the dandy—effeminate men with sensitive hearts and a *faiblesse* for the beautiful.
4. Lury 1996, 152.
5. Williamson 1994, 17.
6. Ibid., 25.
7. This process sets woman at the center of modern consumer culture we would add, projecting her onto a screen that conceals a void at the center of our existence.
8. Williamson 1994, 41.
9. Ibid., 61.
10. Ibid., 62.
11. See Gayle Rubin's seminal article, "The Traffic in Women."
12. Butler 1990, 39.
13. Compare that with how "to cut the melon" is a Chinese metaphor for having intercourse with a woman.
14. Yang 1999, 40.
15. Quoted in Schram (ed.) 1992, 353.
16. Honig and Hershatter 1988, 42. Compare this with how the pigtails of men, a reminder of Manchu rule, were forcibly cut off after the Republican revolution.

17. Four years after she appeared in a *qipao* dress during the State visit, Wang Guangmei, forced to wear a too-small *qipao*, high heels, and a ping-pong ball necklace, was put on public display by Qinghua University Red Guards.

18. Croll 1995, 108.

19. Intentionally, this strategy effectively short-circuited the libidinal economy that had bound together and nurtured society. But only the forced collectivization of the Great Leap Forward could finally disperse the crucial role of the mothers-in-law in China's social fabric (Mann 1994).

20. Meng Yue 1993, 135.

21. Evans 1997, 135.

22. Ibid., 136.

23. Simultaneously, the Western woman, whom China had earlier employed as the symbol of modernity, became the example from which Chinese women should set themselves apart. Western women, it was now said, were commoditized and lacked both discipline and morals (Brownell 1996, 244).

24. See Hakim 2010 or Green 2008.

25. It appeared in 1993 in the section "Mei yu shenghuo" ("Beauty and life") in *Zhongguo funü* (*Chinese women*).

26. Wang Yonghua, "Wo diyici huazhuang zai Riben" ("The first time I used make-up was in Japan"), *Zhongguo funü* (*Chinese women*), October 1993, 29.

27. Fang Yi, "Yizhi hong chungao" ("A red lipstick"), *Shaonü* (*Young girl*), 57 (1995), 24–25.

28. Even in her dreams she is possessed by red lipsticks, putting them to her mouth, clearly an image of the phallic masquerade employed in female beautification and dressing up.

29. See for example Lasch 1979.

30. Compare this with Brumberg's description of the United States in the 1950s.

31. Cheng Ying 1993, 62.

32. Ibid., 63.

33. Ibid. 63.

34. "Yiyan nan jinde" ("It is hard to explain in just a few words") 1993,

35. See Farrer's 2002 anthropological study for more on these phenomena.

36. Liu Ning, "Nüren, bu yao bei qingchun zhuyi suo kunhuo" ("Women, do not let youthism confuse you") 1994, 36; and Chen Yun, "Chi qingchun fan de nühai" ("Girls eating from the rice bowl of youth") 1993, 37.

37. Xiao Li, "Wode xuanze you shenme budui" ("What's wrong with my decision") under the heading, "Guanyu 'qingchun fan' de huati" ("About 'eating from the rice bowl of youth'"), *Zhongguo funü* (*Chinese women*), January 1994, 10.

38. A version of the saying, "Eating from the big rice bowl" ("chi daguo fan").

39. Wen Jie, "Nüxing de qingchun jiazhi he zai" ("What is the value of female youth?") under the heading, "Guanyu 'qingchun fan' de huati" ("About 'eating from the rice bowl of youth'"), *Zhongguo funü* (*Chinese women*), January 1994, 11.

40. Zhang Shuguang, "Yizhong zhanxin de tidai" ("A brand new replacement") under the heading, "Guanyu 'qingchun fan' de huati: laizi duzhe de shengyin (1)"

("About 'eating the fruits of youth': voices from the readers (1)"), *Zhongguo funü* (*Chinese women*), January 1994, 23.

41. Hooper 1994, 73–83.
42. Ibid., 83.
43. Ibid., 80.
44. Evans 1997, 139.
45. Ibid., 139, 140.
46. Ibid., 141.
47. For the following, see Gerth 2003, the chapter titled *Nationalizing Female Consumers*.

Chapter Two

Repatriation of Difference

The rapidly developing Chinese economy discussed in the previous chapters made some commentators feel that tradition was being replaced by a culture of consumerism, lamenting that the political was displaced by the commercial. What, they asked, would happen when the revolutionary ethos was substituted by a capitalist hegemony of commercial popular culture?[1] Others, however, took the view that commercialization and transnationalization would emancipate the Chinese from the State, with some claiming that China's entire ideology would be transformed by soap operas, tabloids, and bestsellers.[2] These would seem to be conflicting beliefs, but in reality they all went back to the same idea of cultural imperialism, where capitalist culture and Western values conflate and where a consumer-oriented economy automatically leads to global homogenization.[3] We find another, more sophisticated approach to this long-standing discussion offered by anthropologist Arjun Appadurai, who argues that globalization involves the use of a variety of instruments of homogenization, such as manners of dress, language hegemonies, and advertising techniques, but that these instruments are absorbed into local political and cultural economies, and *repatriated* as heterogeneous dialogues about national sovereignty, free enterprise, etc.[4] Appadurai makes the important point that the State plays a delicate role as arbitrator in this repatriation of difference. As a result an internal politics of homogenization often plays out in debates over heritage.

This chapter describes how 1990s discourse on femininity shaped such a Chinese cultural politics of gender and identity. We will show how images of women from that decade reveal a shared effort by the beauty industry and the Communist leadership to construct a "modern Chinese woman" where "modern" means investment in beauty while "Chinese" entails an essentialized idea of Oriental femininity.[5] In unpacking the construction of a female

"Chinese beauty," this chapter further suggests that the developing capitalist culture in China moved from a wholesale acceptance of anything foreign in the 1980s to something like a "repatriation" or "domestication" of difference that resulted in values ascribed to Western consumer culture remaining only a surface phenomenon within the discourse of cultural identity.[6]

CHINESE WOMEN'S MAGAZINES

Newsstands in Chinese cities of the late 1980s stocked large numbers of titles geared toward women readers.[7] With few exceptions, they were published by the All-China Women's Federation. Ironically, as was true with other media closely tied to the Communist Party, e.g., China's Central Television (CCTV) and *People's Daily*, the most official and authoritative magazines *Zhongguo funü* (*Chinese Women*) and *Hunyin yu jiating* (*Marriage and Family*) proved to be the most popular with advertisers.

Ever since its founding in the 1930s, *Chinese Women* was the Communist Party's most important forum for constructing and carrying out definitions of women and gender that served a political agenda. The monthly, *Marriage and Family*, was launched much later, in 1984, by the Association for Research on Marriage and Family (*Zhongguo Hunyin yu jiating yanjiuhui*), also under the supervision of the All-China Women's Federation. It served as a forum for discussing and carrying out ideas regarding women and family. In 1995 the monthly circulation of *Chinese Women* was 550,000 and of *Marriage and Family*, 300,000, but since a majority of subscribers were offices and workplaces, these magazines reached a much larger number of readers.[8]

Prior to the 1990s the only illustrations in color in *Chinese Women* and *Marriage and Family* were, like in other Chinese magazines at the time, the cover spreads. The two magazines, which carried around fifty pages of text with a few black-and-white drawings, were printed on rough, darkish paper. When full-page, multicolor advertisements started to appear regularly in the early 1990s, it radically transformed the layout of the magazines. With new sections and articles devoted to everyday life, love, fashion, and beauty, the content also changed. By 1994 advertising space had increased to take up three of the four pages of the cover spreads plus an additional four pages of low-quality mail order ads without illustrations.

As already discussed, Chinese advertising, when it reappeared, was not very sophisticated by international standards. However, with the commercialization of the early 1990s, the layout and feel of the advertisements were increasingly sophisticated, with photos and paper of higher quality. Strikingly the images of women also changed in these magazines, shifting toward an emphasis on glamour, individualism, and hedonism.[9]

The main function of the covers of women's and fashion magazines is to serve as advertisements for the product, that is, the magazine.[10] Covers of *Chinese Women* in the 1980s remained propaganda images featuring serious-looking, working-class heroines in dirty overalls; Party women in blue Mao jackets; or young female soldiers in aggressive poses. From its first issue in 1984, *Marriage and Family*'s covers also were dominated by political messages. They frequently showed mothers or happy couples accompanied by a single child, or young, childless couples holding hands. These covers were promulgating the family planning ideology of the 1980s: fewer kids and later. In the latter part of that decade, however, two things happened that changed the look of the magazines. First the dull cover paper with its bleak colors was replaced by thicker, glossier paper, and second, the images used for covers changed when the Revolutionary representations of the Mao era disappeared in favor of enticing, prettified, fashionable young women.[11]

The covers from then on displayed new, desirable careers for women—Air China stewardesses in sky-blue dresses or young secretaries in front of computers—as well as leisure scenes with women in revealing party dresses, seductive night gowns, designer clothes, and expensive jewelry. Some illustrations broke with conventional role models for women. One showed a young woman in a silky sleeveless evening dress and high-heel pumps, sitting by a bar table with a glass of wine raised to her lips. She is looking straight into the camera, smiling faintly.[12] This was rather risqué at a time when women in general did not drink or smoke, and when frequenting bars was still a pleasure reserved for men.

The interesting thing is how, post-Mao, covers and ads worked in concert to deliver an image of the Chinese woman as a seductive, luxuriating hedonist. Such images reflect a re-feminization that fits well into the idea that globalization leads to a universal consumer culture that propagates Western ideals and values like individualism and hedonism. Similar radical reinterpretations of the Self appeared earlier in the United States and Europe. During the nineteenth century, books and manuals on how to lead a successful life talked of character and were full of words like citizenship, duty, work, honor, and morals.[13] That changed in the first decade of the twentieth century, when individuality and charisma rose in importance. Self-sacrifice yielded to self-realization, and individuality and standing out from the crowd came to matter more than staying in line and obeying orders. Historian Warren Susman talks about a "culture of performers," stressing how the exterior and the visible replaced the focus on intrinsic moral qualities.[14]

An ad in *Chinese Women* for a joint venture company (March 1993) that featured a row of good-looking Asian models illustrates how ideals of individuality and choice replaced collectivity and uniformity in China, too, albeit a hundred years after the West experienced this shift. The women in the ad are dressed in different professional outfits: a business dress, a construction worker's helmet, a nurse's uniform. Others are dressed in sports and leisure wear—one in a swimsuit, another posing as a painter complete with easel, while a third is dressed in shorts and stands holding a football. Smiling and holding on to each other, they all look happy and satisfied with themselves. The ad, which is for sanitary napkins, conveys the idea that women, regardless of the activities they are engaged in, can use Anle pads. But the ad also is an illustration of the changing times. The caption, "The choice of modern women," contrasts the individuality these women embody with their mothers' "choice" of dressing uniformly and being politically correct. Instead of pursuing socialism or the latest Party guidelines, these modern women are pursuing individual careers and lifestyles. None of the models in this ad dons the Mao uniform; instead they flaunt individuality in both work and leisure.

In the first years advertising appeared, the two official Chinese women's magazines, *Chinese Women* and *Marriage and Family*, thus articulated values that are not only usually associated with advertising in general, but also with Western consumer culture in particular. Resembling the West of the early twentieth century, image and mass-consumption culture seemed to contribute toward modeling a new project of the Self that made appearance and image more important than character and collective morality. Furthermore, the changing images of women underscore the thesis that the Revolutionary program was being challenged by a capitalist commercial culture. However, the Chinese relationship with politics, market, and culture was much more complex than this. In the following pages, we will see how the Party and the market simultaneously tout the ideals of a particular, subservient Chinese femininity.

IN SEARCH OF CHINESE BEAUTY

As we saw in the preceding chapter, gender categories in Mao's China were replaced by Revolutionary, class-based role models. The belligerent Cultural Revolution practically outlawed feminine beautification along with cosmetics and fashion. The partial dismantling of the Maoist ideology in the 1980s allowed people a certain degree of individual freedom, including the right to choose how to dress, what hairstyle to wear, and whether or not to use makeup. Femininity that had been repressed resurfaced together with an openly displayed interest in the female body. This interest, however, saw gender differences as grounded in biology, more connected to the Republican Era than to Maoist Revolutionary gender politics.

In the Republican Era, Chinese science tried to ground gender in biology by referring to hormonology. Scientists argued that male hormones created the "air of a man" while female glandular secretions transformed prepubertal androgynous girls into adult women.[15] In young women, physical characteristics like developed breasts and the broadening of the pelvis were thought to be accompanied by distinct psychological characteristics that made women "gentle and soft," "bashful," and "sentimental."[16] In the early 1980s, similar biological explanations of gender surfaced in the popular press. Pseudo-medical articles talked about a difference in brain functions between boys and girls that predestined them for separate work activities.[17] Girls, for example, were said to lag behind men in adolescent intelligence tests. Sub-dermal fat and finer bone structure made them slower and weaker than men, and therefore less suited for certain occupations.[18] Simultaneously, critical voices denounced the "Iron Girl Brigade" as role models for women, while newspaper and magazine articles rejected the idea of gender equality and scornfully admonished women to stop acting like "imitation boys" and "iron women." Chinese women were also warned to stop competing with men in the workplace. When girls grew up, it was argued, the heavy burdens of love, marriage, and childbearing made it difficult for women to pursue careers.[19]

The dismantling of Revolutionary practice in the 1980s meant that gender again assumed its former significance as a social category. Mao's legacy forced an anxious examination of where things stood at the moment. By the early 1990s this gender trouble had become so pressing that it triggered a series of articles in the authoritative *Chinese Women.* The magazine ran a lengthy discussion under the heading, "What is the Beauty of Modern Women?" (*Shenme shi xiandai nüxing mei*) between 1991 and 1992. It opened with a polemical editorial referring to what a Chinese scholar living and working in the United States, Zhao Haosheng, had said while visiting China: "There are no real women in Mainland China . . . in everything from attitudes to looks they do not even resemble women."[20] According to this scholar, Chinese women had lost their "female characteristics" (*nüxingde tedian*) as well as their "proper charm" (*yingyoude meili*). Chinese women, he claimed, failed to understand that their true power lay in their "femaleness" (*nürenwei*). It is important to note that the criticism of Chinese women is voiced by a Chinese living in the United States—someone supposedly familiar with both cultures and knowledgeable about how the Other of the West looked upon China. The *Zhongguo funü* editor expressed full sympathy for the foreign scholar's feelings. He "enlightened" her, she wrote, to realize that,

> modern Chinese women have to once again examine what their sexual characteristics [*xingbie tese*] consist of and become aware of sexual differences

[*xingbie yishi*]. Modern Chinese women ought to fully express their own female beauty.[21]

The response from the readers was reportedly huge, and every subsequent issue of *Chinese Women* in 1991, as well as several issues the following year, published letters and articles summing up the readers' views on the topic of Chinese femininity. Good looks and beauty seemed to be important qualities for modern women, and many readers expressed the view that a good, modern Chinese woman must be beautiful and well-dressed. But even if most of the letters seemed sympathetic to fashionable and beautified women, some called for moderation. One reader wrote that she grew up in a time when "the individual and sexuality did not exist" (*wuwo wuxingde shidai*). She supported the quest for personal beauty, but with the condition that "women should not, as many now do, blindly follow fashion, paint their lips all red, and only wear famous brand-name clothes."[22] Despite disagreements, the readers seemed to agree unanimously on one thing: contemporary Chinese women were too strong and coarse, acting too much like men (*jia xiaozi*). "Strong women" (*nü qiangren*)—an expression signifying women with careers—were definitely not feminine. A woman should not let work or studies make her forget that she was first and foremost a woman, a wife, and a mother. Chinese women needed to become more concerned about their husbands and families.

It is important to point out that although it was someone living in the West who was given the privilege of initiating this discussion, the West did not provide the ideal. The function of the Chinese-American was to introduce the Other's gaze. The important question seemed to be whether the West appreciated Chinese women and if it did, how. Many readers pointed out the differences between Western and Asian women, and made clear they preferred to revive a lost Chinese femininity. Sun Wanqun from Jiangsu, for example, favored traditional ideals of femininity—and readers repeatedly pointed to such qualities—writing that "Chinese women should preserve their Chinese characteristics and, compared to Western women, be more reserved and shy (*hanxu*)."[23] Many letters proposed traits that modern Chinese women should possess: being "soft and gentle" (*wenrou*). One woman wrote that "gentleness indicates the soft and lovable, it is a fine quality for a woman, and not at all a shortcoming."[24] It was because they were not soft, shy, and reserved that Western women were said to differ from and fall short of Chinese women. In short, the consensus was that post-Mao Chinese women should stop acting so assertively. Women were allowed to be good-looking and intelligent, but they should downplay these qualities and pay more attention to serving their husband and child.

Articles in the similarly authoritative *Marriage and Family* also talked about the softness of women. One described how a woman should treat her husband. If he is in a bad mood, shouting and throwing things about, she should tolerate this and try to comfort him. She should then rub his forehead and beseech him, "Tell me what's bothering you."[25] Women were then advised to take their husbands out to karaoke bars and let the men have some fun. The author describes an exemplary woman she knows, a woman not pretty but "soft as water."[26] Every morning this friend of her rises from bed earlier than the husband, boils water, and prepares his breakfast. With a gentle and quiet voice she then asks him to rise from bed and come to eat. The author concludes that these qualities give great charm to a woman and will be of much help in finding a partner.

That other official magazine of the All-China Women's Federation, *Marriage and Family*, later took up the *Zhongguo funü* (*Chinese Women*) discussion on the beauty of Chinese women.[27] The article "China Has No Women" clearly refers to what the U.S.–based Chinese scholar had written in *Zhongguo funü*. The article repeated that a woman should not only be "soft" (*wenrou*), but also "natural and naïve" (*tianzhen*).[28] While modern men do like women who are educated and intelligent, they disapprove when women flaunt these qualities. Women must be "reserved" (*hanxu*) and not show off their knowledge and intelligence. "Nowadays men seldom look for a woman who is stupid, but neither does he like one who takes pride in being clever." Similarly, men do like women who are "pretty and coquettish" (*yaoyan*), but a woman does not have to be beautiful: "A sweet, happy woman can gratify a man because most men love women who, now and then, cleverly say 'thank you.'" What really moves a man, the article continues, is a woman who listens respectfully and with full attention to a man's opinion. In general men also like a woman to show how much she appreciates and worships them. The author says he has never met a man who likes a fearless and brave woman, a woman who speaks in a loud and clear voice, or a woman who tells dirty jokes, gambles, and swears.

To sum up, a good modern woman is someone who focuses on a man's well-being. A self-sufficient and strong woman is unattractive, and can only become a real woman when she makes herself soft, reserved, and submissive. Many of these articles define women's good qualities from a man's point of view, that is, from the male gaze. However, this retrogression of Chinese gender politics was not only about the symbolic or sexual role of Chinese women. It was a backlash in gender equality required by the changing political economy of the 1990s.

About the same time as the ideal of a domesticated Chinese femininity appeared in official women's magazines, Zhu Rongji, vice premier and economy tsar, made the bold move to start dismantling the huge state-owned enterprises (SOE) that, because of their massive financial losses, were dragging the economy down. The result of closing them was massive unemployment.

Those who lost their jobs also lost the entire welfare network that was a part of these SOEs, which had assured married couples that their employers would take care of their children and provide apartments and pensions for both spouses working at state enterprises. Losing their jobs meant those couples lost all of those benefits. This move was difficult for a Communist leadership to execute, and it is clear in hindsight that this action turned the clock back on gender equality. In a biting backlash, women working in factories found themselves unemployed with no choice but to return home to care full-time for their children, husbands, and households. The solution to the restructuring of the economy was to invent in a self-Orientalizing manner the traditional Chinese housewife.

Statistics also clearly show that in these massive layoffs, women disproportionately were squeezed out of the workplace. A 1998 survey showed that in Chinese cities, women, who made up 39 percent of the workforce, constituted 63 percent of the layoffs.[29] Chinese scholar Wang Zhen argued in an article, "Women have been singled out as special targets of the massive layoffs in State-owned and collective enterprises."[30] All-China Women's Federation, at the same time it hosted the much-lauded international women's conference in Beijing, rationalized this gender backlash. As this transformation from a socialist to a capitalist economy took place, they advocated the reestablishment of a feminine ideal of the traditional, subservient East Asian housewife.

ORIENTALIZING FEMININITY

Since the early twentieth century the female ideal for Chinese biopolitics was the Western woman.[31] A recent study shows how in the 1930s representations of women changed radically into that of a more robust, healthy, and strong type.[32] Chinese women who took part in the hard work of liberating the country by force and then, under Mao, moving the backward rural economy into the Industrial Age needed to be strong. But in the 1990s a self-Orientalizing attempt was launched, presenting the ideal "modern woman" as someone who did not "flaunt her qualities." Chinese women were now instead effeminized and portrayed in pseudoscientific terms as weak and passive. The All-China Women's Federation actively propagated what they described as distinctive Chinese or Oriental qualities that Chinese women should possess. This discourse was spelled out not just in their flagship publications. The magazine *Dongfang nüxing* (*Oriental Woman*), which they sponsored, was part of this campaign and promoted Chinese female role models together with articles about Chinese fashion and traditional dress.

To sum up, in official discourse the model Chinese woman was portrayed as someone who served the family, was attentive to her husband and devoted to her child. This female ideal was constructed not only in contrast to men, but also against the Other of individualistic, hedonistic Western women. But what about the emerging Chinese consumer culture we have been discussing? Did it not join with the beauty industry to promote a Western kind of femininity, i.e., individualistic, liberated, and independent?

Yue-sai Cosmetics

American cosmetic group Coty's opening a plant in Shanghai in 1998, in line with Chinese regulations, had to be as a joint venture with a local enterprise. But while this usually meant partnership with a Chinese firm, Coty partnered with Yue-sai Cosmetics, Inc., a leading cosmetic company in China owned by Chinese-American Kan Yue-sai. In the early 1980s China's Central Television Network invited her to leave the United States and run a television show. Both Chinese and American, she was perfect for presenting images from around the world to a nation that had just recently abandoned its isolationist policy. Kan Yue-sai soon became a household name among the Mainland audience, a status she would later cash in on by starting her own beauty product business. That venture allowed her to highlight her familiarity with the world outside China.

Kan Yue-sai willingly gave interviews in all kinds of popular Chinese magazines, as well as contributing regularly to "Half of the Sky," a weekly feminist television show.[33] Her style and look were copied by innumerable women across China. During the 1995 International Women's World Conference in Beijing arranged by Fulian, Yue-sai cosmetics were advertised as an "official" product of that event. This supported her general strategy, which she professed from the beginning was based on altruism and her desire to help China and the women of China. Kan Yue-sai claimed to be driven by two things. First, she wanted to make Chinese women as beautiful as other women around the world, which she would help achieve by instructing them on how to dress and put on makeup. Second Kan Yue-sai strove to change Westerners' misperception of Asian women's beauty. "They think we are exotic but not beautiful," she said. "In a lot of advertisements, they make us look weird. I want to set a standard."[34] Pointing out that Asian women have different skin complexion and facial features than do Western women, Kan Yue-sai created a product line that was made exclusively for Chinese skin.

Kan Yue-sai's further goal was to transform this cultural aesthetic into a beauty politics where female prettification resides neither in heterosexuality nor in narcissism, but in gaining acceptance for China as a member of the rich, Western world. In this process she also managed to reinforce the notion of a particularly Asian skin in ways that echo how nationalist thinkers in the early twentieth century used Western ideas of a "yellow" race to create a stronger Chinese identity.[35] Kan Yue-sai perceived this cultural/national identity to be immutable: "Whether you wear Armani or Valentino, deep inside you are still Chinese," she posited.[36]

Orientalist Advertising Representations

Kan Yue-sai's marketing blend of beauty and identity politics was perhaps most elegantly expressed in a 1994 ad campaign for cologne. In one of these ads, we see the back of an Asian woman dressed in what looks like a white, embroidered wedding gown. She wears a pageboy haircut that reveals a smooth, naked neck sporting a pearl necklace.[37] The image is taken with a soft focus lens that produces a mellow, romantic flavor intensified by the warm, soft colors of yellow and creamy white. The caption reads, "How can you ever forget your first love?" (*ni zen neng wangji di yici ai*). The woman's body language expresses softness and modesty, together with a certain elusive charm that stands in sharp contrast to how women had been portrayed in the preceding ads we have discussed here. This woman seems too shy and reserved to even meet the gaze of the beholder. She turns her head away from the camera so as to not reveal her face. The ad successfully illustrates the notion of a particular Chinese beauty. In a new economy of desire, the woman is portrayed as bashful, modest, and reserved—a deception that becomes apparent when our gaze falls on her unzipped dress.

A similar construction of an apparently shy Oriental woman appeared in a progression of five ads for Simisi, a skin product, published in consecutive issues of *Chinese Women*, also in 1994.[38] The first ad shows a woman's head and shoulders covered with a pink cloth. In this representation of a traditional Chinese wedding, we first see the bride preparing to show her face to the bridegroom. She has started to gently lift the veil with her well-manicured, red-nailed fingers, and only one part of her face is visible—her luscious, red lips. The caption promises to "reveal to you the secret of the women from the South." In the following issue, she has raised the veil a bit further, and now her left eye meets the reader's gaze. In the third ad, her entire face is unveiled and the young woman is smiling shyly. Her head is tilted slightly forward in what looks like the beginning of a respectful bow. The woman is revealed to us piece by piece, using the elegant device of a veil—first her bright red lips, then her left eye enters the portrait, and, in the last ad, the entirety of her face accompanied by the perfectly manicured, long, red-nailed fingers.

In an image from the perspective of the male gaze, the model presents the reader (the gaze of an imagined groom) her attractive femininity bit by bit, turning each part of her face into a separate desirable object. In the fourth advertisement, the woman tries to cover her face again, this time by putting her well-manicured hands over her mouth. In his book on gendered body display in ads, sociologist Erving Goffman calls this gesture "licensed withdrawal"—a move to conceal face or mouth when under the influence of emotions that might risk losing control over one's expression.[39] Is it fear or joy at meeting the groom's gaze that causes the bride's response? Her eyes are still fixed seductively on the one who is admiring her, indicating that any shyness is feigned. In the fifth and final ad, she drops her hands and, with a faint smile, reveals that she was just playing a game of seduction.

The young woman is presented as if the reader were the husband-to-be, anticipating the consummation of their marriage. She is beautiful but also bashful enough to appear to hide her eagerness. The woman's act of unwrapping herself with feigned shyness portrays her giving herself to the groom. Read against the social context of the gender backlash in China of the 1990s, this representation of a traditional wedding becomes more disturbing. Arranged weddings in premodern China were managed by parents, usually against the will of the young brides. So as the state was urging women to leave the workplace and return to taking care of their family, this symbolic display of submission and being subjected to the gaze of the male Other contrasts starkly with the gender-egalitarian appeal of a socialist gender politics.

Simultaneously with the post-Tiananmen, Party-orchestrated patriotic movement described in the introduction, we also see ads becoming more nostalgic. The focus of ads is not primarily modernity, but the very Chineseness of women. Accompanying the five different photos in the Simisi ads are short texts that urge the reader to "Listen for a while, to the legend of silk." The text twists a smooth, rhetorical rope consisting of the "Southern woman's" beautiful character, her sleek skin, the pure silk of her dress, and, finally, the skin-care products, asking, "Why is it that so many women from the South have skin like packed snow, matched with an innate beautiful character?" In another Simisi advertisement, the caption boldly spells it out: "Simisi's women are very Chinese."[40] In that ad, we see a woman in a traditional embroidered dress with wide sleeves and a high collar. With hair artfully arranged, she tilts her head, looking down while serenely playing a flute. The pictorial assertion of the cosmetic company's resuscitation of old gender ideals in a modern society is followed by an ominous, prophetic promise: "From this moment starts the transformation of beauty. Retrace the tactful gentleness, the smoothness, and the clear spirit. . . . Make a very Chinese woman" (*zuo yige hen zhongguode nüren*). With a blatant use of the phallic symbol par excellence—the flute—sexuality and modesty here conflate into a symbol of the traditional Chinese woman: an absent beauty invoked for the political needs of a post-socialist regime.

In general Chinese women certainly did not start to emulate these ads. The women who did dress up like old-fashioned brides or escorts were the "Miss Welcome" girls at expensive hotels and restaurants or KTV venues—exactly the professions where this fashion paired with the promise of pleasure for men.

In a sense these advertisements read like mirror images of the stereotypes of bold Western women we will discuss in more depth in subsequent chapters. A dichotomy is firmly erected between East and West that came through clearly also in discussions with Chinese editors and the creative departments of advertising agencies. In these conversations the "inner beauty" (*neizaide mei*) of Chinese women often was placed against the "outer beauty" (*waizaide mei*) of Western women. The Chinese advertising models consequently embody a certain femininity (or beauty) that resembles stereotypical, Orientalist representations of a woman characterized by a refined, sensual, and submissive desire. The Orientalist stereotype is, however, not the conventional Western fantasy, but rather a consumerist construction that strengthens a Chinese self-identity.

Furthermore, advertising images are clearly ruled by a male gaze. However, instead of a visual language focusing on the display of the body and face—indicating a projection of the Self, ruled by outer qualities such as looks and appearance—the women in these Chinese ads try to make themselves invisible. They seem to retreat into the background, hiding from the attention expected to be shown a woman. While this dovetails well with Western theories of femininity as that which retreats from the male gaze, the concealment of their "outer beauty" here expresses the "inner beauty" of an essential Chinese femininity. The Chinese models in these ads turn their heads away shyly so we can't see their faces, or they cover their faces with their hands or a veil. Superficially we could argue that it is as if by "acting shyly" that they can resolve the contradiction between living up to the narcissistic female exhibitionism of a global consumer culture and the ideal of a submissive Chinese woman. As will become clear in the following chapters on fashion and the changing semiotics of China's ideals of beauty, her disappearance into a dark background of yonder has a more profound significance.

NOTES

1. See Huang 1995, Dai 1999, and Liu 1997.
2. See Yang 1996 and Zha 1995.
3. The awareness of a constantly present West in consumer cultures around the world is, however, something that forces us to reconsider any simple causal process by which the West influences the "rest." Fredric Jameson expressed the situation well in an interview, explaining, "The First World does not have to know the Third World, while it is quite obvious that it is impossible in the Third World not to be aware of the First World" (Jameson 1993).

4. Appadurai 1990, 307.

5. Anthropologist Richard Wilk has a similar take as Appadurai that he expresses in an article about Belize beauty pageants. He writes that these beauty pageants serve the State's interest in "domesticating difference" by constructing a notion of a particular Belizean feminine beauty (Wilk 1996, 218).

6. For a discussion on Western beauty ideals and Asia, see Laura Miller (2006) and Wen Hua (2013) who, writing on Japan and China, respectively, both question any simple connection made between "Westernization" of beauty ideals and such Caucasian features as big eyes, a high nose, an oval face, etc.

7. More on this in Liu Shengzhi 2007.

8. Interviews with editors at the two magazines conducted in Beijing, May 1996.

9. Although the ads with Caucasian models definitely show a lot more naked skin, ads with Asian women in the 1980s also begin to employ nudity and sex appeal when compared with the prior tentative sensuality and cautious display of the body.

10. See McCracken 1993, 14–18.

11. Louisa Schein has commented on how eroticized images of the white woman were used in the 1980s as a way of mediating a shift in Chinese values regarding sex and women, but how in the 1990s, Chinese women recovered this symbolic space of desire (Schein 1994, 152).

12. *Hunyin yu jiating* (*Marriage and Family*), July 1990.

13. See Susman 1984, 280.

14. Ibid., 280.

15. Dikötter 1995, 151.

16. Ibid.

17. Honig and Hershatter 1988, 15.

18. Ibid. 17.

19. Ibid.

20. "Shenme shi xiandai nüxing mei?" ("What is the beauty of modern women?") *Zhongguo funü* (Chinese Women), August 1991.

21. Ibid.

22. Xiao 1991, 22.

23. Sun 1992, 18.

24. "Xinde nüxing yu xinde shidai" ("New women and new times"), *Zhongguo funü* (*Chinese Women*), December 1991.

25. Yao 1993, 22.

26. Ibid.

27. Found in the section, "Nanren zhen xinhua" ("Men Speaking from Their Hearts").

28. Liu 1995, 40–41.

29. Wang 2003, 161.

30. Ibid.

31. See Brownell 1996, 229, for more on the Chinese ideal of the Western body.

32. See Gao 2006.

33. The title comes from the Mao Zedong quote that describes the role of women as "holding up half of the sky."

34. Seno 1998.

35. Dikötter 1992, 124.

36. "Haiwai jiechu nü huaren yingping tianshi Jin Yuxi" ("An outstanding Chinese abroad, the angel on television: Kan Yue-sai"), 1989, 19.

37. *Zhongguo funü* (*Chinese women*) June 1994.

38. *Zhongguo funü* (*Chinese women*) January to June 1994.

39. Goffman 1987, 57.

40. *Zhongguo funü* (*Chinese women*) November 1994.

Chapter Three

Fashion Anxiety

> Why doesn't Chinese fashion measure up against that of the West? Do we never catch up with them?
>
> —*Elle* [Chinese edition] March 1, 1998

As we have already seen, with Mao Zedong dead and China pursuing its Open Door policy of economic reforms, attitudes toward gender and sexuality changed quickly. A beauty industry started to emerge as hairdressers and beauty salons popped up in every little town. Perfumes and cosmetics were ubiquitous on the counters of small shops. Of course this also involved fashion. The unisex Sun Yat-sen suit and military uniform of the Mao era were replaced by a more gender-specific dress code and Western-style clothes, including colorful garments displayed in outdoor markets.

These developments did not come without criticism, however. When the designer house Pierre Cardin staged a fashion show in Beijing in 1979, the *Peking Daily* published letters from "readers" expressing disapproval of how young people were paying too much attention to their looks.[1] "Instead of devoting themselves to work, these young people prefer to wear pornographic bellbottom trousers, get their hair done, and excite themselves doing foreign dances," read one comment.[2] The following year, when American fashion designer Halston staged a show in Shanghai, a Chinese man in the audience remarked that the models belonged in a mental hospital rather than in a fashion show.[3]

However, in the interest of developing a Chinese textile and fashion industry, these critical voices were ignored. In fact, state-owned textile and clothing companies soon started to put on their own fashion shows, and in 1981 the China Silk Import and Export General Company launched a magazine called *Shizhuang* (*Fashion*).[4] To head off eventual criticism, the fashion shows were referred to as "artistic performances."[5] But, in the Anti-Spiritual Pollution Campaign of 1983, Western fashion and adornments were criticized again, and many young people caught dressing improperly or attending dance halls ended up in prison.[6] *People's Daily* told citizens to avoid "bizarre dress," to shave off sideburns and mustaches, and to avoid makeup, earrings, and other "unhealthy" adornments.[7]

When critical statements were made about fashion, they often focused as much on its non-Chinese origin as on its representing capitalist culture. A solution to this problem was made by sorting out which styles could be incorporated into Chinese culture and traditions, and which could not. Defending his trade during the Anti-Spiritual Pollution Campaign, one Chinese clothing designer said: "There is no reason why people cannot wear jeans and colored shirts. . . . Clothing that exposes the bosom, back, and shoulders is not suited to Chinese customs and will not be popular."[8] A renegotiation of values was taking place and on the table was a demand to maintain this new sexual order as Chinese and not to let it become part of a symbolic international arrangement. This seemed particularly difficult because fashion is not only so embedded in a discourse about the new and the international, but also bound to a particular geography of modernity.

Although the image of woman often is used to represent the preservation of a group, people, or nation, beginning in the late Industrial Revolution feminine fashion became associated with modernity and change. Since this happened in tandem with nineteenth-century imperialism, being "in fashion" or "modern" also came to refer to a global hierarchy of symbolic importance. Paris, London, and New York were the centers from which the colonial enterprises were organized, and it was from these Western cities that everything new and modern spread to the rest of the globe—fashion being not the least important of those exports.

China also was caught up in this geographical hierarchy, assigning to Western fashion the status of clothing of wealth and superiority. This was, however, nothing particular to the era of imperialism. Fashion was traditionally bound up with the politics of social class, hierarchy, and what Bourdieu labels *distinction*. As a textbook on twentieth-century fashion puts it:

> Clothes were a tool of oppression, a weapon yielded against the poor. They were used to drive home the lesson that the grand were not simply different; they were better, because they were rich. They wore on their backs the proof that they were superior intellectually, morally and socially.[9]

Because of the historical background of imperialism, much twentieth-century nationalist discourse in China stigmatized fashion as the abject "Other." However, with economic reforms and the emerging consumer culture, fashion, like femininity, reentered the symbolic order as well as the real of China's economy. Since censorship still prevailed and the country had been cut off from the rest of the world, the appearance in 1988 of the multinational magazine *Elle* was an important factor in the reintroduction of fashion into post-Mao China. The magazine's arrival in China furthermore raises an obvious question: How did the magazine's Chinese editors handle the introduction of foreign Western fashion into a country whose ideology was in the process of exchanging Maoist anti-imperialist xenophobia for a nationalistic, albeit globally connected, capitalist culture? To answer this, we will examine the politics of *Elle* in China, analyze readers' responses to the magazine, and interpret Chinese fashion photography spreads from the 1990s. But let us first recapitulate the politics of the female body in twentieth-century China.

GENDER AND THE POLITICS OF FASHION

Together with women's fashion, the female body always was a passenger in the front seat on China's ride toward modernity. The best-known example of this is, of course, the discourse on foot binding, which occurred at a time when China was threatened by the outside world and many feared national extinction. Against an ideological backdrop of social Darwinism, the old custom of binding women's feet was criticized, ultimately not because of the cruelty and pain inflicted but because the practice was said to weaken Chinese offspring. When the bound foot turned up in twentieth-century nationalist discourse, it was as something that set Chinese women apart from the women of the West, who were imagined to be stronger. The mothers must be physically fit to successfully nourish babies they were carrying and so, because women carried the nation's *future* in their wombs, foot binding had to stop. This turned the female body from a semiotic mark of cultural identity into a symbol of old versus new. The female body was from then on a canvas on which to paint the arrival of a future modern China: the site of a political struggle or a metaphor for the social body.[10] The bound foot thus carries both temporal and geographical meanings. Getting rid of foot binding drew China closer to the rest of the world, but it was also a first move toward the appearance of a "new Chinese woman."

Another corporeal symbol of a strong, modern nation was new hairstyles. Beginning with the May Fourth Movement in the 1920s, radical women adopted a short bob. This hairstyle had its roots in the West, where the ideal of an athletic, masculine woman had become popular, but it was part of a simultaneous global phenomenon heralding a new woman and femininity, "the modern girl."[11] This coiffure signified many things for the Chinese:

manliness, freedom, modernity, and the West. In China the bob was even more scandalous than in the West. It evoked reactions sometimes as harsh as those when, at the end of the Qing Dynasty, men's queues fell out of favor. All around the world, bobbed hair came to symbolize women's freedom and equality to men. In China it was condemned as "a symbol of female promiscuity, of explicit sexuality, and of self-conscious denial of respectability and the domestic ideal."[12] There were reports of Chinese Nationalist soldiers cutting off the breasts of revolutionary women with bobbed hair, communicating to women in a language of sexual mutilation that they should not imitate men.[13] But despite cruel punishments and criticism, the masculinization of Chinese women intensified as the twentieth century radicalized and the need for modernization became ever more urgent.

Like in many other countries, Chinese women were not only seen as carrying their nation's future in their wombs but also were made to represent the nation's past. We can see this in something as mundane as tourist guides costumes, which often dress women in traditional clothing of specific countries: the Japanese geisha in kimono or the Indian woman in sari. Likewise we are accustomed to seeing Chinese women wearing the *cheongsam* (*qipao*, as it is called in standard Chinese). The history and original function of the *qipao*, however, has nothing to do with traditional Chinese femininity. When the *qipao* came into fashion in the late 1920s, most Chinese women dressed in jacket and skirt worn over trousers. Although when it emerged the *qipao* was worn as a sign of progress and modernity, its name refers back to "banner gown" that had been worn by the detested Manchu military units. Australian historian Antonia Finnane suggests that the *qipao* was actually an imitation of the *changpao*, a long frock worn by men in the Qing Dynasty.[14] The two dresses were similar originally; by borrowing this outfit, Finnane believes Chinese women were claiming equality to men.[15] In Cantonese, *cheongsam* means long gown, and the name still refers today to a dress worn by men. Suddenly, however, it became part of an attempt to militarize the feminine difference in the service of modernizing the nation. Feminine fashion was from then on increasingly masculine in origin.[16] One could argue that this is a symptomatic paradox of the construction of gender in twentieth-century China.

Men's sartorial plight frequently differs from that of women. They are generally expected to adapt to global fashion and imitate the dominant culture. But when the Communists took power in China, Mao resisted instructions from the chief of protocol to wear a suit and black leather shoes. He instead proclaimed that China would have its own customs and not follow the West.[17] The so-called Mao (or Sun Yat-sen) dress, which consisted of trousers and a jacket that buttoned up to the neck and had breast pockets, became the working garb of New China. In addition to top Chinese leaders wearing it when they met foreign statesmen, a majority of Chinese used this uniform under

Mao.[18] In dark blue or grey, it served as the uniform of workers and cadres, and in military green, it was worn by the PLA and Red Guard students.[19]

During the Cultural Revolution, Maoist attitudes about fashion and female adornment became more extreme. For example, Red Guards roamed the streets, forcibly cutting off women's braids as the only hairstyle recommended for women of marriageable age was now the formerly detested short bob.[20] Armed with guns and scissors, "purification" teams also adjusted people's clothes. Women wearing inappropriate dresses risked being stripped naked in public, thereby making clear the connection between fashion and a fallen woman.[21] Any attention paid to beauty and feminine adornment was considered bourgeois, counterrevolutionary, and outright criminal.

Mao Zedong's primitive understanding of economic matters prescribed a tougher, more aggressive population, as well as a larger workforce. Clothing as well as gender became uniformly male. However, with Mao gone and capitalist reforms coming into being, former ideals were about to change dramatically.

Western haute couture for women had already been introduced in the early 1980s during promotional visits of Pierre Cardin and other fashion houses. But it was only in the 1990s that high fashion got a grip on the Chinese imagination. This process was enhanced by media exposure and also by the "needle trade," in which First World fashion was manufactured in Third World countries. China's fashion industry had been a priority in the country's economic planning since the early 1980s. By the late 1990s, China had already become the world's largest producer of clothing and textiles. One commentator at the time stated:

> Fashion is implicated in the State project of modernization precisely because of its signification of change, and its identification with Western fashion centers, high lifestyles, and, most importantly, an exuberant modern society that China is striving to become.[22]

Historian Antonia Finnane goes even further, suggesting that the Chinese engagement with world fashion reflects "intense national anxieties."[23] If fashion assumed this level of importance for the nation, the question arises of how the Chinese were to learn what international high fashion was all about. The population had been protected from foreign influences for many decades, with knowledge of foreign fashion deemed criminal. In the Reform Era, the notion of fashion (*shizhuang*) turned out to be very popular, but the plethora of styles people wore had initially little to do with international trends. Consumer culture and commercial media became instrumental in furthering fashion knowledge, and beauty articles and advertising were rightly described throughout the 1980s as educational. But when "femininity," "fashion," and "beauty" reappeared in the public discourse of the early Reform Era, there were no media solely devoted to these topics, and magazines run by the Women's Federation produced only occasional pieces on how to dress and present the body.

As part of a plan to develop a domestic textile industry in China, magazines like *Shizhuang* (*Fashion*), published by China Silk Import and Export General Corporation, and *Xiandai fuzhuang* (*Modern Dress*) appeared in the early 1980s. In the 1990s, magazines such as *Nüyou* (*Women's Friend*), run by the Shaanxi Provincial branch of the All-China Women's Federation, devoted large sections to beauty and fashion, publishing in color on glossy paper. These magazines could not, however, compete with *Elle*, the French multinational fashion magazine that entered China in 1988 and was the first foreign magazine in any category to be published in the People's Republic of China.[24]

THE CHINESE *ELLE*

Published in twenty-nine countries and with a total circulation of 58 million, *Elle* was truly a multinational magazine when it entered the China market. Among its eight Asian editions, three were in Chinese, serving Hong Kong and Taiwan before its introduction to the PRC. The PRC *Elle*, also called *Shijie shizhuang zhi yuan* (*The Garden of World Fashion*), initially filled its pages mainly with fashion features from Western editions.[25] *Elle* was first distributed in larger cities because demand there was the highest and circulation most efficient.[26] The magazine began with only two issues per year, and in 1993 increased to bimonthly publication and in 1997, to publishing monthly. The first issue of *Elle* appeared in 1988 in bookstores and newsstands in Shanghai and some other cities.[27] An eyewitness from Hangzhou recalled the crowds and the chaos that erupted as the stack of the first Chinese *Elle* quickly sold out.[28] Beginning in 1997, *Elle* was sold and distributed by the General Post Office, greatly increasing the availability for readers throughout the country. In 1995 the Mainland print run was reported to be 150,000 and its publisher, Hachette, claimed that the magazine sold out as soon as it hit the newsstands.[29]

With a price of 16 *yuan* (approximately $2) per issue—four times as expensive as most Chinese women's magazines at the time—*Elle* was far too expensive, even for relatively affluent urban residents.[30] Despite the high price, most women interviewed claimed they read *Elle* often. As young female readers at the time said, *Elle* was definitely the best women's and fashion magazine in China, and if they could not afford to buy it themselves, they borrowed it from friends or relatives.[31] The high price actually positioned *Elle* more firmly as a magazine for the up-and-coming. One advertising director at BBDO in Beijing explained that although the products advertised were still too expensive, *Elle* was really popular among new urban professionals: "*Elle* is very inspirational, Chinese women in JV's [joint ventures] all read it. They can learn about beauty, fashion, and new lifestyles."[32]

To advertisers in China, *Elle* consequently marketed its magazine as being for "upscale female readers, aged 25-plus."[33] Advertising professionals in Beijing, Shanghai, and Canton attested to success with that target group, claiming that *Elle* was a high status magazine for young successful Chinese career women, such as those working in foreign companies.[34] Marketing director Amanda Turnbull was enthusiastic about what the survey revealed about *Elle*'s readers: "They are open to new ideas, and this can only lead to greater desires and more consumer purchases. . . . *Elle* helps to stimulate those desires and educate women about fashion and beauty."[35] *Elle* did, in fact, function as educational material. It introduced the joy and discipline of fashion and beauty to the up-and-coming women of urban China. This role of the magazine was important for beauty products and fashion houses advertising in *Elle*, but it was crucial for Chinese leaders involved in developing the domestic textile industry.

The publishers of *Elle* liked to claim that their different editions were altered and adapted to the local readership and culture, with the goal of creating truly local editions. Looking at the Mainland China edition of *Elle*, however, it is striking how little local Chinese content it carried. The majority of illustrations of women in the first years, including the covers, featured top models and film stars from the West. How well *Elle* adapted to the local conditions in China also drew mixed reactions. Readers' comments published in the magazine clearly show that many wanted the magazine to become more Chinese. One reader complained that *Elle* lacked local characteristics (*diyu tese*).[36] After all, she said, "*Elle* is ours, it is our 'fashion window to the world' . . . and should propagate and promote fashion designers and models from mainland China." Referring explicitly to *Zhongguo neidi*—excluding Hong Kong and Taiwanese fashion, models, and designers—the issue here was not about race or ethnicity, but about national identity. Another reader who complained about the "elite" approach of *Elle*, argued that since this was the *Chinese Elle*, it must not give up the *minzu* (*national*, referring both to ethnic groups and the Chinese nation).[37] "We have 'one world' first when we include all the various ethnicities and nations," she wrote, obviously referring to *Elle's* Chinese title, *A Garden of World Fashion*. She found that both text and images of *Elle* tended to be "Euro-Americanized" (*oumeihua*), and argued that the proportion of content between East and West must be "appropriate" because "otherwise one could just as well read a foreign edition of the magazine."[38]

While these readers argued for a more Chinese *Elle*, others wanted the Chinese *Elle* to offer a helping hand to China's fashion and clothing industry. The Chinese *Elle*, they proposed, should develop and run more stories on Chinese fashion designers and other Chinese professionals so they would become better known in the "outside world."[39] Another reader wanted the magazine to create a special section for Chinese designers, expressing her wish that Chinese design take a place on the international scene and that Shanghai become one of the world's fashion centers.[40] In the 1980s, Tokyo had managed to join this handful of international fashion metropolises in a business otherwise dominated by Europe and the United States.[41] The Chinese fashion industry hoped that Shanghai would copy that feat in the 1990s.[42]

The readers not only wanted to study Western fashion, they also desired to reconnect to a Chinese traditional aesthetic. To accentuate this, they expected *Elle* to help Chinese designers to transcend China and spread Chinese fashion around the globe. Such a wish might at first seem strangely displaced.[43] The thing to remember, however, is that since *Elle*'s inception in the late 1980s, it played a special role in Chinese State-led attempts to establish a domestic fashion industry for export. That was obviously why Hachette, as the sole foreign publishing house operating in China, was allowed to start selling the magazine. The owners of *Elle* developed good enough connections in China to host their own international fashion show parties at the Diaoyutai State Guest House, a venue used by government officials for State dinners and banquets when they received international political leaders.[44]

That the new expensive magazine was going to be something of an instruction book for Chinese tailors was acknowledged by *Elle*'s publisher in China, Lo Chaotien.[45] *Elle* became China's window to the international fashion world, or, as stated in the Chinese title, "the garden of world fashion."[46] Readers who worked in advertising and in fashion and clothing production clearly understood this function, admitting that they used *Elle* in their professions. One fashion design student expressed her concern that Chinese fashion designers would not be able to produce their garments in a timely way since *Elle* presented seasonal fashions according to the calendar. Her solution? That *Elle* move up the schedule of its content, showing summer fashions already in the spring issue.

The propagandistic/commercial function of Chinese media became clear as *Elle* brought together the nationalistic propaganda discourse of the time and the local fashion industry.[47] We can see this in *Elle*'s eventual introduction of the Chinese models and designers called for by readers, as well as in how the magazine framed local stories in a nationalistic narrative. For example, when the designer Wang Xinyuan was interviewed in 1994, the article started by comparing the tough competition in the fashion world with sports, saying that it took great strength (*shili*) to fight one's way onto the Italian fashion scene, especially since "fashion is not one of China's strongest areas."[48] Wang described his ambitions, saying that he had worked with people all over East Asia and always wanted to be known more widely. He asked rhetorically,

"When will I ever be able to break out of East Asia and make it in France and Italy?" Wang, who grew up in a military family and has General Patton as his role model, served in the propaganda unit during his military service.[49]

We find a parallel story to Wang Xinyuan's in a piece on Chinese designer Zhao Weiguo (his given name translates as "great country").[50] Zhao was the chief designer of the State agency for the development of Chinese fashion.[51] The apex of his career came when he was chosen to represent China at the international fashion show in Shanghai. A foreign designer there walked up to Zhao, took his hand saying: "Your stuff is good. It can surely be sold internationally." The writer commented: "He did not let us down. He gave face to us Chinese (*zhengleguang*)!" We see the importance here of the foreign Other and also sense something of the "intense national anxieties" Antonia Finnane associated with Chinese attempts to create a fashion industry.[52]

The photograph that accompanied the story on Zhao Weiguo covered two pages and illustrated well the conflation of Chinese fashion with notions of progress, modernity, and the future. The scene shows eight female models standing on a rooftop, wearing clothes of his design. In the near background is a high-rise building under construction with cranes and construction platforms clearly visible—something that probably would have been avoided for a Western audience here displays its full symbolic value. Women and fashion here signify a promised future, replete with urbanity, affluence, and international recognition. Female fashion coded nationally and temporally is literally equated with constructing the new China. Fashion becomes exactly what it means in most European languages, namely, *la mode* or the "modern." But as we shall see, it also involves a nostalgic return to the past. The fashion spreads in *Elle* were eventually accompanied by stories and images that wove traditional Chinese culture into a discourse on international relations and modernization.

DOMESTICATING SARTORIAL DIFFERENCE

It is important to point out that the expression "world fashion" used in the Chinese name of *Elle* has connotations contrary to concepts such as "world music." Instead of denoting Third or Fourth World fashion, it refers to European, American, and Japanese haute couture. Therefore all fashion features in the early issues of the Chinese *Elle* were Western-produced. However, perhaps in response to readers' demands, the magazine eventually began introducing Chinese-produced material. The interesting point about this material is how it negotiated the gap between what was considered foreign fashion and the models, who not only were Chinese, but expressed the particular Chinese femininity already discussed above. One such feature, eight pages long, was titled, "Sounds of Autumn in the Divine Land" (using the poetic term *Shenzhou* to mean China). In melancholic photos, we see a young Chinese model posing outdoors in clothes by local designers.[53] As in most Chinese productions, the models do not show any of the playfulness, sensuality, or energy often displayed in Western fashion spreads, striking instead shy and melancholic poses. In poetic language, the text introduces the illustrations of the *Shenzhou* fashion spread by describing how

> the Divine Land of China has without noticing it slipped into autumn. The photographs introduce Western clothing and self-produced dresses. In this moment the images are blurred, making it impossible to detect anything artificial.[54]

The melancholic atmosphere that accompanies this story on autumnal nostalgia—the loss and withering of old China—rings true with the models' appearance. What follows is a bit more mysterious—what is meant by "images are blurred, making it impossible to detect anything artificial"? A clue appears on the next page of the article. After introducing the autumn of old China and the blurring of the past and the present, the superiority of Chinese aesthetics is laid out in a patriotic vein, with talk about the "mild and indirectly tactful . . . the pretty and charming" nature of this fashion, and how "natural and harmonious" it all seems. These qualities give fashion a whole new content. The foreignness of Western fashion is effectively repatriated, the difference absorbed by a Chineseness that serves both as an aesthetic notion and a particular perception of femininity.

In January 1996 another fashion feature took up a similar theme. This time the title of the eight-page feature was "Spring Sun at the Ancient Capital of the Six Dynasties." The illustrations were from the Purple Mountain Observatory outside the historic capital, Nanjing, and the text accompanying the photographs used time, history, and space to speak about fashion:

> The daydreams follow each other at the Purple Mountain Observatory. Three hundred years after the English Industrial Revolution, Marks & Spencer waits impatiently for the confidence of the Chinese girls [*guniang*]. English fashion seems even more elegant on their bodies than on the English girls. . . . The extragalactic stellar systems seem closer than ever. The earth belongs to the universe. How can one then distinguish between fashions across different national borders? The spring sun rises in the east and the twenty-first century belongs to Asia.

Beginning with images of Chinese imperial history and science, and moving on to the European Industrial Revolution, the text concluded by claiming China's right to the fruits of modernity. In this circular mode of presenting history, China would regain its former glory, somewhat magically, by appropriating fashion. When Chinese women, who are more feminine than "English girls," dress in Western style, something extraordinary happens—the clothes look better. Echoing the international media hype of the time, the passage ends by stating that the twenty-first century will be Chinese.

However strange those ruminations on Chinese history and the future may seem in a context of seasonal fashion spreads, they are not isolated instances.[55] This nationalist rhetoric of fashion and femininity appears frequently, as, for example, in an article by Fu Yaomin that featured clothes by Gibierre and Chinese designers.[56] The photographic images of this fashion spread were set in the former living quarters in the Imperial Palace in Beijing and displayed various combinations of clothes, all red. The title, "Fashion Portraits Below the Forbidden City," leads off an article whose atmosphere is also melancholically nostalgic. Making a poetic attempt to come to grips with the contradictions inherent in China's modernization process, the text weaves a now familiar fabric of Chineseness, femininity, the world, and the future.

> Whether in our days or in the past, whether in China or abroad [*gujin zhongwai*], blood red is a positive color. It symbolizes hope and represents happiness. It is soft and warm. Women in our country wear a red wedding dress when getting married. Santa Claus, giving presents, does likewise. . . . See how well the clothes harmonize with the ancient Forbidden City. See how smartly they match the Chinese girl. Each and every item draws the contours of the 1990s.[57]

Elle was not alone in using the Forbidden City for fashion shots. Designer Hu Xiaodan also staged exhibitions in the Forbidden City, proclaiming, "No matter how deeply the Forbidden City is tinged with feudal belief in the supremacy of imperial power that put the wealth of the whole nation into one person's hands, it is still the crystallization of China's genius and wisdom."[58] These fashion spreads shot in the Imperial Palace, the Purple Mountains, the Ming tombs, and other ancient places and buildings, show how important it had become to reconnect with a lost Chinese universe.[59]

The narratives about the Chinese fashion designers in the articles analyzed above are similar in their discussion of China's successful appropriation of the foreign, all embellished by a nostalgic celebration of a glorious Chinese past in which beauty reigned supreme. The meeting of Western fashion and Chinese genius now leads to a third culture, not a hybrid of Western and Eastern, but something inherently Chinese. The whole point is that Western fashion simply looks better on Chinese models. Does this not sound like another manifestation of the century-old vision of how to reinforce Chinese culture with the help of Western technology, echoing the self-strengthening motto from the nineteenth century—use what is Western for practical matters while keeping the Chinese essence? Obviously the patriotism campaign following the Tiananmen massacre had penetrated even consumer culture, advertising, and fashion discourse.

Wrapping Western fashion around a national essence embodied by woman is not just for saving China; it has turned into a predictive indicator that says the twenty-first century belongs to China. The modernity of dress becomes in the Chinese discourse a futurology turned fashion, a prophecy about a coming Chinese century. These women emerge from a background of historical sites and imperial palaces that represent an eternal China; only they, the Chinese models, are able to accommodate and pacify the otherness of fashion. There is not so much a self-Orientalism at play here as a repatriation of difference. Chinese women do not change, but fashion does, and when fashion finally settles on its rightful owners, it generates a culture more feminine and refined than any such sartorial culture of Western origin.

NOTES

1. As is often the case about the PRC, it is hard to say here what is a genuine opinion voiced by someone in the public and what is edited.
2. Quoted from Schell 1986, 154.
3. Ibid., 156.
4. For more on the Chinese fashion industry, see Tsui 2010 and Wu 2009.
5. Stross 1993, 250.
6. Read Liao Yiwu's multivolume "Interviews with People from the Bottom Rung of Society."
7. Ibid., 253.
8. Quoted from Schell 1986, 166.
9. McDowell 1984, 10.
10. As Susan Bordo (1993) and Mary Douglas (1970), respectively, theorized this phenomenon.
11. See the 2008 text *Modern Girl around the World* by Alys Eve Weinbaum, Lynn M. Thomas, Priti Ramamurthy, Uta G. Poiger, and Madeleine Yue Dong.
12. Sun Lung-kee 1997, 357.
13. Ibid., 361.
14. Finnane 1996, 113.
15. The cut of the *qipao* changed radically. Originally a dress covering the body, loose down to the ankles, wide, and long-sleeved, by the 1930s it started appearing as a sexually revealing dress, cut at the side up to the hips, sometimes sleeveless (Ng et al. 1994). The *qipao* came in the West to be associated with prostitutes, especially after the film *The World of Suzie Wong* (Clark 1999, 160).
16. However, China was not fully the "country of blue ants" Western media often portrayed it to be. People were not forced to wear a uniform as some commentators claimed, but the strong frugal ideology did not accept too strong an interest in individual dress or style (Wilson 1999, 174). In 1956 there was even a short-lived

campaign to liven up the monotone and drab female fashion (see Finnane 2008, chapter 8).

17. Finnane 1996, 99.

18. This Mao suit was not Chinese at all but modeled on early twentieth-century Japanese student uniforms copied from the military uniform, in turn borrowed from the Prussian military.

19. After the mid-1980s, top CCP leaders shed their Mao uniforms and appeared in Western-style suits.

20. Honig and Hershatter 1988, 42.

21. Steele 1999, 59, 60.

22. Li 1998.

23. Finnane 2005, 589.

24. This was done in a joint venture with the Shanghai Translation Publishing House.

25. The magazine marketed itself to advertisers as *Elle China.*

26. Kunz 1996, 328.

27. Ibid. 327.

28. Interviews conducted in Shanghai 1996.

29. See "Mainland women willing to absorb fashion trends," 1995, and "*ELLE* grows despite tighter local market," 1993. Such statements on publication figures were unreliable in China at the time, but the popularity of *Elle* was demonstrated to the author in interviews with advertising directors, magazine editors, and a number of young Chinese women in Beijing and Guangzhou in April 1996.

30. *Elle* originally cost much more than domestic beauty and fashion magazines. This gap eventually closed somewhat; in 1998 *Elle* cost sixteen *yuan*, the domestic fashion magazine *Shizhuang* (*Fashion*), twelve *yuan*.

31. Interviews undertaken 1995.

32. Interview Guangzhou 1996.

33. A&M, Feb. 24, 1995.

34. Interviews conducted in 1996.

35. "Mainland women willing to absorb fashion trends," 1995. A survey conducted in 1994 by the magazine produced similar results, showing that its readers were generally optimistic about their future (ibid.). The same survey revealed two other important things: Chinese readers were very positive toward advertising and they had high disposable income because most still lived with their parents.

36. *Chinese Elle* 1998 (4).

37. *Chinese Elle* 1998 (10).

38. These cultural definitions of fashion as distinctly national are linked to essentialized constructions of Western and Chinese femininities. Establishing a correspondence between the bodies and manners of Chinese women and Chinese fashion, one reader wrote that the "sophisticated, elegant, modest bashfulness" (*dianya hanxu*) of Chinese fashion corresponded nicely with Chinese women (*Chinese Elle* 1994, 5). Chinese women were said to be just as "delicate, soft, and smooth" as Chinese fashion itself. On the other hand, the writer concluded, the character of Western women fits hand in glove with the exaggerated "bold and unrestrained" fashion often displayed in the Western editions of *Elle*.

39. One Chinese reader who was working in an Middle Eastern country wrote that she would like to have found Chinese designers and clothes based on a "traditional Chinese aesthetics" in foreign editions of *Elle* as well (*Elle* 1997, 11), stating that the outside world needed to see what the many-thousand-years old culture could produce when it came to fashion.

40. *Chinese Elle* 1998 (6). The reason behind this was that she strongly wanted Chinese clothing to enter the global stage (*zouxiang shijie*).

41. For an account of the Japanese fashion industry's international rise to fame, see Kondo 1992.

42. Finnane 2003, 602. In her 2008 book on Chinese fashion, Finnane is quite pessimistic about China's chances, especially in the short term, of becoming anything other than a provider of clothes designed by foreigners. She blames an obsession with national essence that had influenced fashion shows since the 1990s. With fashion constantly referring back to China's glorious sartorial epochs in history, she found creativity to be lacking (Finnane 2003, 281–283).

43. There is, of course, also the possibility these postings might have been written by the editors.

44. Hachette was equally sensitive to adverse conditions in China, canceling a feast scheduled during the disastrous flood catastrophe in 1998 and halting production temporarily after the Tiananmen massacre in 1989.

45. See Baughman 1988.

46. Illustrations in Chinese magazines and ads were often "borrowed" from *Elle*, and turned up in many domestic Chinese women's magazines, either as editorial illustrations or in new advertisements. The Western imagery of *Elle* was also put to use in more concrete ways. For example, a young female student in Beijing I met posted illustrations of Western women from *Elle* on her university notice board to advertise her Avon parties. In a Beijing record store that sold mostly pirated foreign hard-rock CDs, the long-haired shopkeepers had decorated the walls with images of Caucasian models from *Elle*. *Elle* became something of an image archive of Western images that were reused and recoded locally.

47. See Zhao 1998, 98. As we saw earlier, advertising brought about a commercialization of media that was not only accepted but was, in fact, encouraged by the leadership. Although the Chinese media now had to rely on advertising revenues and sales, they were still expected to function as an active propaganda organ for the Communist Party, establishing the unique phenomenon of "propagandist/commercial" journalism.

48. *Chinese Elle* 1994 (4).

49. Tsui 2010, 35, 36.

50. *Chinese Elle* 1994 (4).

51. The first generation of Chinese fashion designers seems to have been all men.

52. Finnane 2005, 589.

53. *Chinese Elle* 1994 (5).

54. This distaste for artificial, fake, unnatural, un-Chinese surfaced, as Karl Gerth has shown already, in discussions on femininity in 1930s China with women advised to be "authentic" and to not behave like prostitutes (Gerth 2003, 306–8).

55. That England, the imperialist enemy from the Opium War and a "century of humiliation," is singled out in this sartorial discussion on modernity and culture is in itself very interesting. But on the other hand Marks & Spencer is big still in post-colonial Hong Kong.

56. *Chinese Elle* 1995 (6).

57. Ibid. Observe how this short text and others emphasize that these are *Chinese* women.

58. "Beauty and the East," 1995.

59. Many of the fashion shows staged around the country contained explicit references to China's history and the dresses of the various dynasties (see Finnane 2005, 605).

Chapter Four

Breasts, Modernity, and White Skin

Fair skin was already a hallmark of beauty in China in ancient times. It signified membership in the aristocracy, while dark skin indicated that a person belonged to the large majority of poor working peasants. Under the impact of global consumer culture, the meaning of skin color has been recoded. A hairless and smooth complexion is constructed as that body characteristic that foreigners lack and appreciate. The smooth skin of women became a sign for "Chineseness" and functions as a last layer of protection against the hostile outside world. The skin must be kept intact lest the vital essence of Chinese identity be lost.

While the beauty ideal of fair skin is indigenous to China, the ideal of large breasts came from the West. It became popular as a sign of "modernity," first among the *demi-monde* of the Western-influenced treaty ports and then, after having been suppressed under Communism for three decades, among the young women of the Reform Era. In ads for bust enhancers in the first half of the 1990s, a large bust signifies a Western Other who is free, independent, and seductive. Unlike the models in the ads for whitening creams, who stay indoors and nurture their beauty in order to please their husbands, the women in bust enhancer ads are depicted in outdoor settings, thoroughly enjoying their own sensuality. At the same time, bust enhancer ads also compare women to flowers and bushes in the idiom of archaic fertility rituals of the spring, with phallic connotations numerous and obvious. The protruding breast becomes a symbol, a fetish, to erase the visible proof of difference that exists between the self and the Other, and invested in a hope of what the economic reforms and Open Door policy will eventually harvest.

BREASTS

In an article on China's popular attitudes toward the West in Republican Era treaty ports, anthropologist Virgil K. Y. Ho describes how breasts in China were traditionally considered unimportant to a woman's attractiveness.[1] Only beginning in the 1920s did large, unbound breasts become a symbol of sensuality and feminine health. In the trading port of Canton, buxom courtesans became popular to the point of being adored.[2] Western women's large, natural breasts were openly praised and seen as an ideal for all Chinese women.

> Physically, "natural breasts" symbolized better hygiene and health. Culturally, they became a symbol of women's liberation from "feudalistic" bondage. Politically, they were seen as an efficacious "Western means" of creating the kind of strong and healthy Chinese race urgently needed to strengthen the nation.[3]

Traditionally breasts were tied flat to the body and, even in erotic paintings, often remain covered by a *moxiong*—an undergarment fastened tightly at the back.[4] In early twentieth-century China, parallel to the "natural feet movement," nationalist reformers launched a "natural breasts movement."[5] While the natural feet movement set out to do away with the painful tradition of breaking young girls' feet and turning them into tiny "golden lotuses," the natural breasts movement was in favor of abolishing the custom of tightly wrapping women's chests. This old practice, the reformers believed, prevented breasts from fully developing. But while the movement against bound feet was tremendously successful, the natural breasts movement was abandoned early on.

Despite the otherwise radical gender politics, a moralistic attitude aimed at repressing what pertained to sexuality and the female body remained in Mao Zedong's China. In addition to working, dressing, and looking like men, wearing short hair and loose-fitting Mao suits, women were expected to conceal their feminine curves. As we have seen, with Deng Xiaoping's economic reforms and the Open Door policy, the female body was again eroticized. The ideal of a large bosom, first introduced in the foreign-influenced treaty ports, was thus revived in the 1990s with a veneration of large breasts that was at least as strong as in the 1920s.[6] Demand for products and procedures believed to increase the size of breasts therefore appeared in various forms.[7]

BUST ENHANCERS

Women's magazines in the 1990s also abounded with articles and ads focusing on breast enlargement. The methods ranged from massage, creams, medicines, and bras, to cosmetic surgery.[8] The most popular device was the bust enhancer that came in different forms and was sold by mail order and in larger shops for between 60 and 400 *yuan* (approximately $7 to $45).[9] The most common type consisted of a plastic cup to be put on the breast, a hose, and a pump. The massage given by the pumping device was to increase blood circulation that, it was claimed, would result in a bigger bust.[10] A variant of this was a battery-run enhancer, which was marketed as being more practical than the pump. "It's like a new form of bra," the ad reassured potential buyers. "It can be worn working, traveling, or while doing housework. It is so quiet that not even the people standing next to you will notice it."[11]

In the mid-1990s the magazine *Nüyou* (*Women's Friend*), which targeted teenage girls, devoted most of its back-page ads to various bust-enhancing products. Published in Xi'an by the All-China Women's Federation of Shaanxi province, *Nüyou* was the fastest-growing and best-selling magazine in its category at that time.[12] It was so popular that knock-off issues bearing *Nüyou*'s name started to turn up regularly on newsstands.[13] To a large extent, *Nüyou* consisted of light material, covering topics such as love, relationships, lifestyles, beauty, and fashion. But it also held a considerable number of more politically correct articles about working women, women politicians, and revolutionary veterans. The magazine was very popular with advertisers, who had to buy ad space more than a year in advance.[14] Since the bust enhancer is a product targeted at young women, it is in magazines such as this that we find the most bust enhancer ads. Every issue of *Nüyou* in 1995 carried them.

The adoration of large breasts was a relatively new phenomenon, and in the discourse of advertising and beauty articles, breasts are associated with the West, civilization, modernity, and naturalness. Just as in the West, notions of breasts in China are highly polysemic. Breasts are said to stand for everything from motherhood to femininity to good health to sexual attraction. Chinese skin care ads, as we will see in an upcoming discussion, represented nature as malicious. In contrast to this, bust enhancer ads from 1995 associated breasts with health and nature. In skin care advertisements, women were portrayed as trying to protect themselves from nature and were advised to not venture outdoors. In bust enhancer ads, however, nature is represented as pleasant, healthy, and beneficial.

In early 1995 most ads for bust enhancers actually showed women in a sunny outdoor setting. While the sun in ads for whitening creams was presented as the main threat to women's beauty, in bust enhancer ads, it is a source of pleasure and well-being. In an ad for Eve (*Xiawa*) bust enhancers, we see a young woman reclining on an outdoor terrace.[15] She is sunbathing with her face turned toward the sky, thoroughly enjoying the return of the warm sun after winter. She is surrounded by a number of brick and cement pillars topped with protruding conical things. Inserted in the image of the woman and the phallic structures is a poem about Eve and the Garden of Eden that also refers to the sun.

At this moment,
Apart from the sunlight,
There floats around me
A recollection
It has already drifted through a thousand universes.
Through the ages of history
The thought flutters like a bird
As my memory touches on a myth
I sing again
About the beautiful legend
About Eve,
About Eden

The poem's reference to the Garden of Eden evokes the innocence and purity of nature before the fall. While the function of the phallic cement constructions is apparently to provide shelter from the sun, the young woman is evidently not interested in protecting herself. Quite the contrary, she lies with her head flung back, exposing a naked throat, her face turned toward the warm April sky. Wearing just a sleeveless top and short skirt, her body clearly enjoys the caress of the sun. Sunbathing was not a popular pastime in China, but this woman enjoys it, oblivious to the devastating effects it will have on her skin.

Other ads by the same company similarly convey an image of nature as benevolent. In one ad, a woman is seen caressing her chest and throat, head flung back in pleasure.[16] The text advises women to start caring about their bodies "so that the spring and summer of 1995 will give you the bright and beautiful sunshine, the pure and fresh air, and all the happy people you hope for." The sun and the fresh outdoor air are seen as good for women's bodies, making them grow and develop.

Frequently portraying young women against a background of trees and bushes, bust enhancer ads compare women with trees and flowers. The brand *Qiaojianxiong* (the Quiet Bust Enhancer) is a good example. One of its ads shows a young woman standing in front of a shrub with the sun shining down on her face and breasts.[17] Raising one elbow, she pushes her bosom forward. A short poem with the title, "Meeting with Spring" (*Yuehui chuntian*) uses the image of bushes in springtime as a metaphor for the maturing of a young woman:

> The days are sometimes warm, sometimes chilly. The withered stems are sprouting anew. A curtain of green mist is reflected in the eyes. One easily sees the spring trembling at the end of a branch.[18]

Just as bushes grow in spring, so a woman's breasts will blossom with the help of the bust enhancer, an apparatus that, the ad suggests, has the ability to replicate the powers of nature.

Bust enhancer ads portray women in harmony with the natural environment. They participate in the changing of seasons, like plants that sprout and grow in the warmth of the spring sun. The bust enhancer's function is to assist nature, and its powers are presented as similar to those of Mother Nature, even in ads that set women indoors. Sunlight is always present, often falling through a nearby window on the models' faces and chests.[19] The impression is created that the sun—as a giver of life—will somehow make breasts grow bigger. Larger breasts are a sign of a higher level of energy, and the logical conclusion is that a woman with big breasts possesses more vital strength than does a flat-chested one.

CONFUCIUS AND THE FEMALE BODY

Apart from comparing the growth of breasts to the blossoming of flowers and trees, many bust enhancer ads also engage a discourse on modernization, in which a large bust signifies a more advanced stage of civilization. In an ad for "the device that builds a beautiful and large bust" (*jianmei fengru qi*), we see a black-and-white drawing of a buxom young woman with her arms raised behind her head, fully displaying her chest. The text reads,

> A well-developed bust and graceful curves are the visible signs of a woman's youthfulness and vitality. As mankind prospers and society becomes more civilized, more attention is paid to such matters. In response to the demands of our times and in accordance with the special biological characteristics of the female sex, our factory has consulted foreign advanced technology and manufactured the Beautifying Bust Enhancer.[20]

Breast size becomes a reflection of a social and technological level of development and is explicitly linked to prosperity and civilization. The popularity and prevalence of large breasts in the West are explained by advances in modern medicine and science *plus* a more advanced stage of civilization. Some advertisements also draw a direct connection to the technological and scientific achievements of the West by tracing their bust enhancers back to nineteenth-century England:

> Rudimentary brassieres were first made in England a hundred years ago using silk and iron threads. A century later, bust enhancers have developed, from merely satisfying some very simple demands of women to also giving them

> psychological satisfaction. This has been done by "weeding through the old to bring forward the new."[21]

Ending with a well-known political slogan of the time the manufacturer claims its bust enhancer gives Chinese women "psychological satisfaction." In a pseudo-Marxist manner, the attempt is also made to connect a particular beauty standard with a certain historical stage of development. Breast size becomes a marker of universal modernity, turning bust enhancer ads into a Chinese discourse on modernization, the West, and national identity. The ad claims that a rich and civilized society pays more attention to female curves, suggesting that breasts are an indicator of a society's maturity and development. While in the West, modernity and large breasts go together, the lack of large breasts in China is blamed on China's peculiar politics of beauty:

> As a result of deep-rooted, Confucian ethics, people in ancient times did not allow full, round breasts or plump and round buttocks. Because of this unreasonable morality, the "beauty-building" [*jianmei*] of our women was halted. However, with women in Europe and North America, the opposite was the case. At all times have they have done whatever it took to get a fit and beautiful body. This is especially true for the bust, which can be said to be the true manifestation of "fitness and beauty." Fortunately, in recent years our female compatriots have come to fully understand the importance of a full, firm, and protruding bosom: a full bosom is an unrivaled symbol of feminine attraction. Breasts are not just something for babies to suckle on. They are also the most important criterion for judging a woman's beauty.[22]

This "unreasonable morality" of Confucianism that hindered the development of female curves also obstructed China's modernization. Obviously referring to China's economic reforms and Open Door policy, the text rejoiced in the fact that Chinese women had come to understand the importance of the female figure. Through physical training and bodybuilding, it was feasible for Chinese women to catch up with their Western sisters. When it came to the display and beautification of their bodies, Chinese women would liberate their "true selves" by casting aside traditional Chinese morality.

> Whether in the sunlight of the day
> Or the floating shadows of the night
> In those moments that belong to yourself
> Take off your traditional Chinese skirt [*hua chang*]
> Let your true self [*zhenshide ziwo*]
> Roam freely
> On the outstretched earth
> An intoxicating woman
> The ripe logic of beauty[23]

Women were urged to discard their "Chinese skirt," that is, symbolically cast off their old-fashioned views of the body, and discover their "true selves." Having long been repressed by Chinese tradition, they would now be liberated by the bust enhancer and as the poem proposes, roam freely throughout the world.

These ads suggest that by using a bust enhancer, a woman becomes part of nature, accumulates vital energy, and joins in the cosmic processes of growth and maturation. On the other hand, bust enhancers are also associated with science, technology, and the advancement of modern civilization. While these images may seem contradictory, the ad for the Eve bust enhancers easily combines them. References to the Garden of Eden simultaneously conjure up associations of naturalness and Western civilization. Western civilization's strength apparently is its use of technology to enhance what nature has given to humankind. It somehow liberates the natural energies buried deep within Chinese women, energies long imprisoned by Confucian morality. Western culture is the embodiment of values and forces that are simultaneously immensely alluring and, as we will see with the whitening cream discourse in the following chapter, dangerous. The model in the ad described above is attractive precisely because she evokes these feelings. She has cast off Confucian morality and returned to an Eve-like state, revealing her *true* self as being closer now to nature than to culture. Her seductive voluptuousness is both attractive and threatening, just like the modern Western civilization with which she is associated. Moving over to the ideal of a fair skin we encounter a much different corporeal politics.

COLOR AND CLASS

An article in *Wall Street Journal Europe* from 1996 described how the two global giants of the photo-processing industry, Kodak and Fuji, were engaged in a battle for the potentially huge Chinese market.[24] Fuji had the upper hand because its film made human skin look whiter. Its marketing strategy had successfully taken advantage of the traditional East Asian view that fair skin indicates a high social status while dark skin is associated with a subservient position. Kodak, whose main market was the United States where the current ideal was a deep suntan, doctored its film to make skin look more tanned than it actually was. In order to compete with Fuji, however, Kodak declared that although it did not believe that fair skin was still a class marker in East Asia, Kodak film would be adapted to make skin look paler than it really was.[25]

Fuji was, of course, spot on in its strategy. White, hairless, and blemish-free skin has long been praised by the Chinese.[26] The old Chinese saying, "A fair skin overshadows three ugly qualities [*yi bai zhe san chou*]," clearly attests to this admiration. In ancient China, fair white skin was a symbol of refinement and indicated that a person did not belong to the peasant classes that toiled under the sun. Already in pre-Qin China, laborers were therefore called "black-headed people," marking the symbolic distance between landlords and farmers.[27] Pale skin was a mark of aristocracy, just as long fingernails and lotus-feet would be in later periods. The seventeenth-century playwright Li Yu elaborates on this, arguing that the beauty of fair skin can only be maintained and enhanced if a person is born into the upper classes. Aristocrats are naturally fair-skinned and beautiful, but if they lose their high social position, they lose their beauty as well. And it was totally hopeless for a girl born with a dark complexion to travel the other direction.

> If girls of this kind (neither dark nor fair by birth) are well-fed and if they spend much of their time indoors, their skin may become lighter since their basic color was not entirely dark. . . . But if the natural element in a girl is dark without a light component, she cannot hope to become lighter, even if she took ground rock crystal or cloud mother as a medicine, and even if she lives in jade palaces or agate houses.[28]

With the arrival of a Western imperialist modernity, this Chinese beauty standard of skin color was supplanted, first by a European racial discourse saying Chinese belonged to the "yellow" race and later, during the Mao era, by a dark-tanned face, symbolic of the peasants and workers representing the new politically correct ideal.[29] While the traditional Chinese contempt for peasants was turned upside down under Mao, any positive regard for manual work again vanished after Mao's death. Urban citizens in the 1990s refused jobs as cleaners, waitresses, and construction workers, leaving those tasks to the large masses of migrant laborers from the countryside. In the context of China's rapid urbanization, the urbanites' disdain for manual labor and outdoor work could be interpreted as a fear of losing status, of slipping down the social ladder. Tanned, dark skin had become the sign of the *internal* other, of the migrant laborer living and working in the city without a residence permit. Fair skin—formerly a mark of aristocracy that showed its bearer to be a member of a privileged minority of scholar families—became a trait that separated an urbanite class that was similarly privileged in the modern context from the majority of countryside farmers who were shut out from permanent urban citizenship by the strict *hukou* household registration system.[30]

Both Chinese and multinational cosmetic firms were thriving because of the growing demand for skincare products; this category came to comprise the majority of ads in women's magazines.[31] Multinational cosmetic companies began to move into the China market as soon as the early 1990s.[32]

Japanese firms had extensive experience in the skin whitening business before coming to China. Shiseido could therefore present its exclusive "Beautifully White" (*Meibai xilie*) product line, a set of no fewer than four different products that included whitening emulsion, whitening lotion, whitening softener, and whitening cream. European companies, despite having no home markets for these products, also joined in the competition. Estee Lauder, for example, launched a "Swiss Whitening" line, containing UV protection cream, powder cleanser, mask, and lotion. High-class, expensive products like these were promoted and sold in major Chinese department stores, and advertised in beauty magazines such as the Chinese edition of *Elle*.

Editorial content about beauty in women's magazines from the 1990s elaborated on how to obtain, preserve, and enhance fair, smooth skin, agreeing that dark, rough skin should be avoided at all cost. The articles were hypocritically ambiguous. The following piece, which questioned the white ideal, also confirmed that this was actually still the most desirable skin tone.

> In many people's eyes, a dark face is a defect you cannot plead innocence to, and therefore many people with a somewhat dark-skinned complexion rack their brains to find ways and manners to achieve a whiter face. By painting over their own faces, those eager to have white skin acquire a "false face" [*jia lian*]. With snowy white cream they cover over the black and a rough skin becomes smooth. However, under the layers of whitening powder, the pores look even rougher and acne protrudes more visibly. Add a throat not powdered in white but still yellow or black, and the effect makes a flat face look immensely comical.[33]

Another article appears to trivialize the importance attached to white skin in the same ambiguous way by pointing out that there are beautiful and ugly people in all races, regardless of their skin color.

> There are no fixed rules that define black as ugly and white as pretty. Ideals like these are subject to change. In our country we have the popular saying, "A white skin overshadows three ugly qualities," but we also share an appreciation for dark beauty [*heiliqiao*]. This is exactly as in the rest of the world. There are different races of people: white, yellow, red, brown, and black. Among every race there are those who are beautiful and those who are ugly. You cannot possibly say that all white people are beautiful! . . . To date, there are still no medicines or cosmetics that can permanently change dark skin into white. But this does not mean that dark-skinned women are destined to remain unable to become beautiful. Dark girls can make themselves charming and attractive in other ways. They can, for example, exercise their bodies to become healthy and good-looking.[34]

WHITE SKIN AND PROSTITUTION

So even though fair skin is not a sufficient condition for being beautiful, dark-skinned women still have to compensate for their deficiency by shaping their bodies with exercise instead. Despite the reference to *heiliqiao,* dark skin is in no way regarded as beautiful. Both authors above obviously contradict themselves, first questioning race-based ideals of skin color but then unabashedly promoting and confirming the preeminence of white skin.

This situation, however, becomes more complicated with the intrusion of a global beauty imagery of Caucasian models in magazines, films, and soap operas. The white skin of Western women is established as the ideal, as stated in an article titled "Mistakes in Putting on Make-up."

> If you want to rival the white-skinned beauties of Europe, you cannot avoid having to put on many layers of make-up to successfully cover over your yellow-brown skin. In reality, nothing is perfect in its every aspect, and similarly, no single woman is a perfect beauty. Women from the East [*dongfang nüxing*] admire the snow-white skin of Western women, but on the other hand, do not Western women admire the tender, smooth skin of Oriental women? Be careful about putting on too much whitening cream because it can't change the user into a white-skinned beauty [*bai pifu de meinü*].[35]

The article's tips about the do's and don'ts of using makeup reformulate the ancient Chinese ideal of white skin by presenting the looks of Western women as the ideal. Here white skin does not signify just class and wealth in a domestic context; it is also used to construct identity in a globalized culture. Instead of signifying identity in relation to an internal Other, as it did before, it now constructs a difference against an external Other of the West. The pursuit of beauty is reshaped into worldwide competition where Western women—whose pale skin is supposedly admired by Chinese women—are said to admire the tenderness and smoothness of Oriental women's skin.

It is that imagined judgment of a Western gaze that is valued here. Another article, from the official women's magazine *Zhonguo funü*, applies the same rhetoric but describes Chinese beauty by referring to what foreigners are believed to admire.

> Chinese women have a nice figure. Japanese women really admire the long and slender bodies of Chinese women. The skin of Chinese women makes American and European women exclaim with admiration, "Why has God given them such fine, smooth skin without any thick body hair?"[36]

Chineseness is here not only constructed through a contrast with Western women as the Other, it also becomes a way of creating identity from an external viewpoint. The gaze of the Other is made an arbiter for the beauty of Chinese women, a logic that appears in many different contexts. For example, a Chinese play at the time (based on a book whose author spent four years as a student in the United States) contained a scene in an American home in which a Caucasian-American woman shaves her legs and explains to the Chinese nanny that American men like Eastern women's hairless limbs.[37] Leaving aside the question of how the woman would know this, female beauty here has become a subject for national pride and self-identity. Replacing the focus on skin color, the reference is now to the smooth and hairless qualities of a woman's skin. The original Chinese semiotics of skin color is thus recoded in the global consumerist context of the 1990s. Initially signifying class identity, it begins to represent ethnic, cultural, and national identity as well. Skin is still important for differentiating an imaginary East from a similarly imaginary West, but the shoe is now on the other foot, and skin complexion comes to function as a signifier also for gendered cultural identity.

As we have seen earlier, ads for skin care products and whitening creams from the mid-1990s frequently employed images of women that referred to premodern and early modern China. These images drew on pre-Revolutionary gender values of submissiveness and softness. One example was the six-piece series for Simisi cosmetics discussed in the previous chapter. A bride is here referred to as *jiangnan nuzi* (a woman from the southern economic and cultural center of China's history) in representations of a young woman in traditional Chinese wedding dress with a veil over her head.[38] The text also speaks of silk reelers' hands being smooth and fair. Silk, of course, is a reference to Chinese culture. The veil and the pink dress also are certainly signifiers for traditional Chinese culture and a remark on specific gender relations that defined femininity as domesticity and subservience.[39]

Other skin care ads also employed representations of domesticity, marriage, and traditional gender roles. The company Taitai (*married woman* or *Madam*) ran a campaign in 1995 for Taitai Liquid, with advertisements on television, billboards, and in magazines. One ad showed a bride standing in a church with flowers in her hand.[40] Her white, Western-style wedding gown reveals a high-collar Chinese *qipao* underneath. She looks away a bit sadly and the caption reads, "Glowing with youthful looks." By using a not-so-young looking model and a text about how ugly the skin becomes with age, the ad conveys two messages: first, the importance of getting married before it is too late and, second, the fear that after marriage one's fair smooth skin will deteriorate rapidly. Beauty is fleeting and in order to keep your husband, you must keep your skin youthful, white, and smooth.

Beauty articles and ads from the time, nonetheless, frequently advised women to be careful with whitening creams and avoid using them excessively. Despite these warnings, the models in these illustrations often had faces painted completely white. Another ad for Simisi, and its China Cream, for example, showed the extremely white face of a woman, emerging like a white ghost from a black background. She reverently holds the product in her folded hands. The tagline, written in an archaic seal scripture style, says, "Make plausible a woman's dream." A similarly ghostly ad, this one for a cream aptly called "Bai" (*white*), shows a large close-up of the left side of a woman's face that covers almost the whole page.[41] The face is absolutely pallid and if not for an open eye that shows signs of life, the image could be mistaken for the head of a corpse.[42] The tagline, printed in large characters, advises, "So as not to be vulgar [*tuosu*], be careful not to overdo it," while the pseudo-poetic accompanying text emphasizes the warning.

> If you want to show your true qualities, then do not gloss and whitewash to cover things up. If you seek perfect beauty, do not escape from your own self. If you want to attain eternity, you do not have to worry about the moment. Pure white should not be a morbid pale but should let beauty, fresh and lively, shine through.

The warning against vulgarity in applying whitening cream is interesting since it points to an important theme in most discourses on female beauty: the reward for and the risk of attractiveness. There is a continuation here to what had already surfaced in the Chinese anti-Western discourse of the 1930s following the first inroads of a global consumer culture. As Karl Gerth has shown, the national consumption movement then conflated with the attacks on the so-called "modern Chinese women" in a fear of prostitution and foreignness.[43] Prostitution, which in the 1920s and 1930s increasingly came to be seen as a hindrance to Chinese modernization, was now connected to foreign goods, female beautification, and modern fashion. Modern Chinese women, visible after leaving the formerly so cherished seclusion of their homes were now under the spell of the foreign. Although modernization was needed and women had to partake in lifting China from its sorry state of affairs, the West remained a threat, and as the national commodities movement pointed out, trade was war. If China chose to purchase products imported from the West, they would again suffer defeat. Gerth quotes one of these warning voices saying that because prostitutes wore foreign dresses, one should call all women who did the same "prostitutes." The term "prostitute," Gerth summarizes, "became a twin marker for social decadence and imperialist penetration."[44]

On the one hand, as we have seen above, skin care is in the 1990s similarly constructed as a key to a successful heterosexual love relationship (preferably marriage), but a woman who uses excessive whitening cream or other makeup risks being deemed not only morbid, but also vulgar. In fact, overapplication of makeup is often associated with prostitution, which is highlighted in the following beauty article.

> There are two kinds of women who like to apply thick and colorful make-up [*shenzhuang yanmo*]. The first category comprises those who use a sexy appearance [*sexiang*] to make a living, the other is those women who are engaged in some kind of artistic profession. The use of make-up by those who depend on a sexy appearance for a living is exaggerated to the point of being bizarre. Most people consider the thick and colorful make-up of these prostitutes, dancing girls, and bargirls as a way to make them look seductive and sexy, all in order to attract more customers. In reality this is a problematic question. An alternative explanation of why they exaggerate their make-up is that it can effectively hide their own true self. It makes them look like somebody else. This may not so effectively deceive other people, but they certainly fool themselves.[45]

This article, connecting excessive whitening with prostitution, is remarkable when compared to the previous quote that warned against using too much whitening cream and other makeup when trying to look like a white-skinned European beauty. The implication is that Western women have loose morals. Applying too much whitening cream is associated with sexual promiscuity and is regarded as both immoral and un-Chinese.

THE CHANGING SEMIOTICS OF BEAUTY

Seeing how Kan Yuesai constructed a qualitative difference in skin between East and West, it is natural that an old Chinese ideal of white skin has to be recoded in the consumer culture of the 1990s. As proof of not having to work the fields, it signified an aristocracy of the peasant economy, and the tanning of the skin thus represented social standing or class. This was true also in China where fair white skin was considered beautiful. The 1990s in China saw the age-old social demarcation between the rural and urban population being reinvented once again, with the rural population allowed into the cities only temporally as immigrant workers lacking the basic rights of the urbanites. The socially inflated beauty ideals that reemerged were however complicated by the other foreign intrusion in the urban imagination. White skin now also became an issue of ethnic and cultural identity. In Chinese beauty discourse this paradoxical situation is reflected upon and given a solution as the formerly domestic class ideal is resignified in the new globalized context. The Chinese ideal of a white skin is renegotiated from just being the class marker of white versus dark, to being transformed into another discourse on the hairless smooth skin of Chinese women. It is still a Western, or colonial, gaze that rules the ideal, but in this way cultural identity is retained as difference is safely re-created and domesticated. The theme of skin care ads was not so much how to get a fair skin as the fear of losing it. The fear of one's skin becoming darker can of course translate here into a newly ascending Chinese middle class's fear of falling socially, but we can also in the new global setting of the beauty ideal read this allegorically. Various potions were sold to protect its wearer from the detrimental effects of the sun, wind, and atmosphere on the texture and color of their outer selves. Looking at the images of skin care and whitening products, the models are almost always portrayed against a dark background; shining like a moon in the night their faces radiate with a light that seems to emanate from their innermost power. The advertising rhetoric then talks about protecting this essence, keeping it in, not letting the climate drain it of its vital force. Needless to say the advice to stay indoors reverberates with the earlier admonitions that the beauty of modern Chinese women lay in returning to the home.

The meanings of breast differ markedly, taking an inverted position when it comes to national identity, modernity, and the West. In China the bound, flattened bust was the ideal right up until the last century when some of the treaty ports courtesans made a large bosom fashionable. With its Occidental connotations reform activists at the time saw large breasts as an important ingredient in the construction of a future strong and healthy nation, and just like the liberated foot, they propagated for the unbound breast. Maoist gender politics in its characteristic praxis of combining a liberating discourse with a masculinization of the Chinese body did its best to hide these liberated breasts, in a flattening out also of gender difference. This changed in the early 1990s when a plethora of bust enhancing products appeared on the market: various electric or hand pumping machines as well as potions to either drink or apply to the breasts. Beauty editorials also gave tips on various exercise and massage programs that would enhance the bust. That bust enhancing products were the most visible beauty products together with skin care merchandise makes it even more interesting to note the inversed discursive relation between how the two ideals were presented. Most striking about the bust enhancer ads are the phallic representations and the sun worship. Women in these representations are not interested in protecting themselves from sun and wind. They are seen exposing themselves to the sunshine, taking in as much as possible of the warmth. Taking in the sun (yang) is compared to not letting out the moon (yin) in the white skin ads. Together with the fertility focus in breast ads, there appears a discussion on the modern, on China's development and the West. The assumed poor state of the Chinese breasts is here blamed on Confucius, while the fuller Western bust is seen as a direct effect of the technology and sound ethics of modern society. So, one wonders, is all this work of massaging, exercising, taking in the sun perhaps not about liberation of the female breast, but instead a rigorous discipline to compensate for a lack of potency in the body national? While skin care is about preserving the essence, large breasts become the project of evolving into the modern Other, of Western technology, somehow perceived as natural. That at least seems to be the case when we turn to compare representations of Western versus Chinese women in Chinese consumer and popular culture.

NOTES

1. Ho 1991, 87–104.
2. Ibid., 92.
3. Ibid.
4. Images showing men's chests were more common. It was believed to be a sign of good fortune for a man to have a well-developed chest. See Eberhard 1986, 48, and Kam Louie 2009 for more on male representations.
5. As Anthonia Finnane explains in *Changing Clothes in China*, the liberated breast, the natural foot, and the bob hairstyle were all linked together in an image of a modern Chinese woman who put the survival and the regeneration of the Chinese nation first.
6. This appreciation of breasts and women's desire to have a big bust seems to exist in most of contemporary East and Southeast Asia. In 1993, a Japanese clothing manufacturer made a survey on beauty ideals in eight East and Southeast Asian capitals. Women responded to questions about their body weight and measurements, together with what their ideal measurements would be. All shared a desire for a larger bust. Beijing, the capital in the region with the least developed consumer culture, reported the smallest breast size as an ideal. The other two Chinese cities of Hong Kong and Taipei, with their very developed consumer culture, showed a desire for the largest breast sizes. See "Yazhou nüxing xiankuang diaocha dagongkai" ("An Investigation into the Current Situation for Asian Women Made Public"), *Nong* (I), February 1994, 149–52.
7. Both popular and highbrow literature took pleasure in renditions of breasts and the emotions they supposedly evoke in men. Ai Bei, for example, describes in one novel how, "Her rounded breasts, which jiggled slightly with each breath she took, were taut and soft at the same time; they inspired envy and jealousy in women and nearly uncontrollable passion in men" (Ai Bei 1990, 119). See also Nobel laureate Mo Yan's novel, *Big Breasts, Wide Hips*.
8. Although breast surgery was not common still in the 1990s it has now, with cosmetic surgery in general, become one of Chinas' fastest growing businesses. See Wen Hua for more on this.
9. Despite the high price and the dubious character of this product, business was good for the manufacturers of bust enhancers. Sichuan Chengdu Huangzhen Medical Mechanical Works sold enhancers worth RMB$2 million in 1997, with a sales

forecast of RMB$8 million for 1998. See Pamela Yatsko, "Pleasure and Profit," *Far Eastern Economic Review*, January 29, 1998.

10. A similar belief in the possibility to enlarge female breasts was found in the American female consumer culture of the 1950s. Joan Jacob Brumberg, in her book on the genealogy of the Western body project, mentions how American teenage girls studied advertisements in the back of women's magazines for exercise programs and creams that promised to make breasts grow. See Brumberg 1997, 117.

11. *Nüyou* (*Women's Friend*), February 1996.

12. A director at BBDO/CNUAC Advertising Co. Ltd. in Beijing told me in an interview in April 1996 about a survey they had conducted in 1994–1995 that showed that the readers of *Nüyou* (*Women's Friend*) not only liked the articles in the magazine but that they also greatly enjoyed reading and looking at the ads.

13. This problem with counterfeit copies was discussed in *Nüyou* (*Women's Friend*), November 1995, 10.

14. BBDO/CNUAC interview, April 1996.

15. *Nüyou* (*Women's Friend*), April 1995.

16. Ibid., May 1995.

17. Ibid.

18. Ibid.

19. See for example *Nüyou* (*Women's Friend*), February 1995.

20. *Hunyin yu jiating* (*Marriage and Family*), June 1987.

21. *Nüyou* (*Women's Friend*), March 1995.

22. Ibid., May 1995. Caucasian models were never used for these bust enhancer ads.

23. *Nüyou* (*Women's Friend*), March 1995.

24. "Photo Opportunity Kodak, Fuji Face off in Neutral Territory," 1996, 1, 7.

25. Ibid., 7.

26. As the geisha with white-painted face reminds us, fair skin was a beauty ideal throughout the whole of East Asia. The same ideal dominated much of pre-twentieth-century Europe, changing only when an outdoor recreational lifestyle for the affluent made a suntanned complexion popular.

27. According to Frank Dikötter, this symbolic distance and the contempt for black slaves and peasants tilling the fields under the burning sun was later projected on the world outside China, creating the polarity "between white, the centre of the civilized world, and black, the negative pole of humanity" (see Dikötter 1992, 10–12).

28. Wolfram Eberhard's translation (1971, 279).

29. Dikötter 1992, 8.

30. *Hukou* is a household registration system that has a long history in China. During Mao Zedong's rule, it was used to control every move of the citizens, since they needed permits to leave the community their *hukou* assigned them. Today the *hukou* system is still in effect, and although Chinese urban citizens have a large degree of freedom to move, it effectively stops people in the countryside from settling permanently in the cities. Although they might have been working there as migrant laborers for many years, they are not entitled to attend publicly funded schools or use other services to which those with city *hukou* are entitled.

31. In the 1980s women's magazines had a wave of ads for Chinese-made skin whitening products that promised to conceal all skin flaws and turn yellow and dark

skin white. Some creams even boasted that they would make the skin white as jade in just a week.

32. Skin care products ranked number five among various product categories marketed in China in 1997. US $64 million was spent that year on skincare advertising. In 1996, Elegbacae Depigment Cream had the fifth-largest advertising budget among all companies marketing in China, according to "Top Global Ad Markets," *Advertising Age International,* May 11, 1998.

33. The paragraph continues: "Actually, a dark skin is not such a deficiency. Is it not the case that a great number of dark-skinned *(hei)* women are called 'black peonies' *(hei mudan)* or 'black roses' *(hei meigui)*? One could therefore advise not to make dark skin appear white." The author of this piece questions whether dark skin is such a deficiency and condemns the use of artificial means to make skin paler as attempts to create a "false face." There *are* some dark-skinned beauties, the author points out, as if confirming that the majority of dark-skinned women are ugly, but does not, in fact, deny that fair skin is the beauty ideal to which women should aspire.

34. Zhou Fanlin, "Hei fuse ren de meihua jiqiao" ("Beauty techniques for dark-skinned people"), in the section titled "Jinghuaben C" ("Exquisite selection C"), *Nüyou* (*Women's Friend*), 1993, 99.

35. Lin Lin, "Huazhuang de wuqu" ("Mistakes in putting on make-up"), *Xiaofeizhe* (*Consumers*), January 1994, 13.

36. Zhang Yunjie, "Wo kan yangniu yu Zhongguo guniang" ("Looking at Chinese and Western young women"), *Zhonguo funü* (*Chinese women*), June 1995, 47.

37. Yatsko 1996, 58.

38. *Zhongguo funü* (*Chinese Women*), January to June 1994.

39. We can see this connection between marriage and white skin elsewhere in East Asia. Beauty salons in Japan offer full-body whitening treatments for brides. A wedding night treatment with solutions of vitamin C, licorice extracts, and mulberry roots promises to make the bride's skin "glow with a child-like purity." See Alison Dakota Gee, "The Price of Beauty." *Asiaweek*, August 2, 1996, 40.

40. *Nüyou* (*Women's Friend*), June 1995, 64.

41. *Hunyin yu jiating* (*Marriage and Family*), August 1991.

42. *Zhongguo funü* (*Chinese Women*), February 1995.

43. For this and the following, see Gerth 2003, 304–7.

44. Gerth 2003, 306. One thing that revealed these women as being prostitutes was that they powdered their legs (Gerth 2003, 307).

45. Yu Yan, "Nüren de huazhuang" ("Women's make-up"), *Hunyin yu jiating* (*Marriage and family*), February 1996, 43. The same logic seems to apply to perfumes. A director of an international advertising agency in Shanghai told me that most Chinese women were afraid of using cheap perfumes since they could be mistaken for prostitutes. According to the director, women believed they did not run this risk if they use expensive, foreign, or well-known brands.

Chapter Five

The Love of Western Women

Seen as enemies of the Chinese people from the Boxer uprising in 1900 up to the Cultural Revolution, Westerners were portrayed as child-snatchers, counterrevolutionaries, and spies. In a late-1990s interview, the female author Anchee Min told a blonde, blue-eyed, female reporter that if she had met someone with those features during the Cultural Revolution, she probably would have killed her. With the economic reforms and the opening of China to the outside world in the 1980s, representations and fantasies changed dramatically, revealing the flipside of this relationship, that is, everything Western was adored and coveted. Chinese popular culture from then on was saturated with imported American television shows and films that delivered images of a rich and beautiful West. The most prevalent image was that of the blonde, blue-eyed woman Anchee Min would have killed during the Cultural Revolution. This Caucasian female filled Chinese-produced television soap operas like "Foreign Babes in Beijing" or "Russian Babes in Harbin." She lent her traits to the Chinese dressmaker dummies and adorned magazine covers, posters, calendars, and advertisements. The image of the blonde, blue-eyed Western woman no longer triggered the urge to kill; that xenophobia shifted instead to the other side of the phobic object, namely, a fetish.[1] The white female thus became the prime obsession in a new symbolic universe that was governed not by class struggle and resistance to imperialism, but by the symbolic exchange of a globalized commodity culture.

This became all the more clear in China's developing consumer culture. Since the construction of the Self is closely bound to the Other, advertising creates difference as well as the promise to become someone else, someone worthy of the gaze of the Other. This is a performative promise that takes on great importance in the context of global marketing and advertising. Marketing professionals often reduce the choice regarding using models of different racial and ethnic features to a question of either showing local models so people can identify with them or using foreigners to give a sense of prestige and quality to a product. Caucasian models are used to represent the West. When Caucasian women in ads represent the West, *how* they represent the West is interesting. Although the image of the white woman is always locally re-signified, it also constantly carries connotations of power and pleasure.

The purpose of this chapter is to discuss the Chinese understanding of Western women by examining print advertising and popular culture from the 1990s in the face of fantasies of cross-cultural sex. We will see that Chinese representations of white women not only conflate xenophobia with commodity fetishism but also transcend the usual grid of heterosexual logic that still governs most gender representations. Following literary critic Homi Bhabha's ideas on race, power, and desire, the following discussion suggests that Chinese representations of Western women are a form of racial fetishism.

FEMALE MASCULINITY

There has been widespread concern that advertising objectifies and portrays women as submissive. In this gender construction, men are represented as active doers while women are passive receivers of their actions. As John Berger writes in *Ways of Seeing*: "Men act and women appear. Men look at women. Women watch themselves being looked at."

The concept of fetishism has been used extensively to label this role of women in Western visual culture, describing sexual attraction for female body parts such as the lips, legs, or feet, an attraction that also dominates the imagery of consumer culture. Female representation in Western visual culture has further been defined as a spectacle constructed around a male gaze. In the famous article by film researcher Laura Mulvey, this idea reaches fruition by using the Freudian term scopophilia to describe how gendered representations in film are structured by male fantasies and fears of castration.[2] The Western regimen of gender representations elaborated on by these theories might have changed, but they are still helpful as tools for examining how Chinese women were represented in postsocialist commercial visual culture.

As seen in previous chapters, the body language of Chinese models in ads expressed shyness and subordination with canting of heads and bodies, reclining poses, and covered faces.[3] Chinese models were often portrayed in a childish way, made to act as girls. The image of the Chinese woman thus conveys most of the "feminine" characteristics and also the "male gaze" believed to have once ruled Western visual culture.

Interestingly, this post-Mao re-feminization appeared alongside the masculine representation of Western women. We can trace this phenomenon in the list of gendered body postures sociologist Erving Goffman established after studying Western advertising from the 1970s. These represent women as subordinate, fragile, and childish.[4] Chinese advertising during the first decades of the Reform era portrayed Western women as the total opposite. Rather than bending their knees submissively, women stand squarely, legs straight and wide apart. Instead of inclining their head shyly forward or to the side, they hold their heads high. Gazes are not turned away; rather, Western women look straight into the camera, boldly meeting the eyes of the beholder. Nor do these women cover their mouths when they laugh. If any one thing is characteristic of Chinese representation of Western women, it is their conspicuous laughter; they are shown frequently with wide-open smiles, showing off rows of white teeth. This is extraordinarily uninhibited in a China where any woman who did not cover her mouth while laughing was committing a *faux pas* in most social contexts. Caucasian models do not lower their heads, nor do they lie down in these images. In short, Western women are not portrayed as subordinate. On the contrary, they display the same bodily postures displayed by men in Western advertising, postures that Goffman translates as unashamedness, superiority, and disdain.[5] The Caucasian models in these ads hold their bodies erect and their heads high. They look powerful, self-confident, and self-satisfied.

To sum up, ads with Western and Asian women present two contradictory sets of representations. Asian women are subordinate and childish, while Western women demonstrate masculine qualities of acting as in power and with self-confidence. Furthermore, advertisements featuring Caucasian women belie Berger's notion of "men act and women appear" by showing women doing things with men.

In the Chinese sample, portraying women and men together was rare in ads with Asian models but more common in those featuring Western women. In one ad a man with shirtsleeves rolled up stands attentively behind a Caucasian woman who is dressed in a power suit and has her feet up on her desk.[6] It would appear that the woman, who holds a remote control in her hand, is scrutinizing a business presentation made by the man—a reversal of conventional notions of the male gaze. A similar interpretation can be made of a medical ad that also portrays a man and a woman. A smiling girl in a bathing suit and hat leans over a man lying on a dock.[7] If the former example portrayed gender reversal in the workplace, the reversal in this ad is in the area of sexual initiative. It illustrates the typical beach flirtation, but it is the woman initiating, not the man, who is lying down, which is, of course, a conventionalized expression of sexual availability.

Not only are Western women portrayed as active and powerful, they also present a strong physique, fertility, passion, and sexual activity. Caucasian women are shown engaged in sports and outdoor activities far more often than are Chinese women. They appear on the beach, windsurfing, or on the tennis courts. This portrayal of Western women as athletic tallies well with an earlier-held Chinese belief that the Eastern woman was not as strong as her Western sister and, therefore, unsuited for some sports.[8]

The use of Caucasian models to market clinics and medicines that claimed to cure infertility was another demonstration of the vigor of Western women. The director of a Qingdao clinic, one ad told the reader, had been given the nickname The Child-Bringing Goddess (*songzide guanyin*). The ad features a Caucasian mother sitting beside a bathtub populated with no fewer than five healthy-looking, white children.[9] The four small boys and one girl are all laughing and playing in the water.

In these representations of Western women, the Chinese imaginary definitely is not ruled by a male gaze resulting from male traumas caused by fantasies of female de-masculinization. These women, paradoxically, occupy the symbolic position of having the phallus. Explanations of the female position of both pleasure and power in the examples above need transcending standard heterosexual interpretations of the fetish and the pleasure of watching. Feminist scholar Anne McClintock, for example, deconstructs the Freudian Oedipus myth, showing that fetishism has to do not only with traumas surrounding gender and genital categories, but also with a crisis in the meaning of other social categories such as race, power, and social class.[10] To fully understand the image of the Western woman, we must examine racial and cultural stereotypes to see how they are employed in a Chinese libidinal economy.

OCCIDENTALISM

The laws governing Chinese advertising prohibited nudity from the shoulders to ten centimeters above the knees. In the 1990s, however, this law was strictly applied only to television commercials. Ads in magazines were full of scantily dressed women. Not only were Caucasian models more revealed than Chinese models in these ads, they also were more overtly eroticized. Some of these ads were quite sexually explicit. An ad for a water heater, for example, shows a woman wearing only a short, translucent top that had been ripped to pieces.[11] The image, shot from behind in semi-profile, almost fully reveals the model's naked buttocks. A strong jet of water spurts up from beneath her. The woman's head hangs back as if she is in the throes of great passion, with her eyes closed and her mouth wide open. The caption printed above the woman reads, "With *Qianfeng* (*Vanguard* [the brand name]) in the house, there is happiness" (*jia you qianfeng le zai qizhong*). Another striking example is an ad on the back of *Shaonü* (*Teenage Girl*), an inexpensive magazine for girls in their early teens. In this otherwise cautious and prudish magazine was a photograph of a young blonde woman whose two large breasts are clearly visible through her net blouse. Her pose is similar to those of models in men's magazines.[12] In line with this eroticization of Western women, seminude Caucasian models were used frequently on packages and ads for Chinese medicines and potions that claimed to cure impotence.

In discussing these images, young women in Beijing and Guangzhou in the mid-1990s sporadically referred to the Western models in the ads as *hao piaoliang* (really pretty) or *zhen meilide* (so beautiful), and explained the presence of so many Caucasian models simply as a matter of their being beautiful. The reason for the prevalence of Western women in ads was that Westerners were considered to be the standard of beauty. Advertising personnel and magazine editors commenting on images like these also talked about the beauty of Western women, often creating a dichotomy between China and the West. A middle-aged female director at the Chinese advertising agency White Horse Advertising Limited (*Baima Guanggao Youxian Gongsi*) in Guangzhou explained the frequent presence of Western women in ads by saying:

> Really! In the Chinese mind we think that white women are sexier than Chinese women. And that is maybe the explanation. . . . In our minds we always think that in bygone times Chinese women really had a beauty, an inner beauty, as women. But in modern society white women have all the charms of sex and love.[13]

Explaining female beauty in this way, the ad director could mean a number of different things. She could be saying that in modern society, white women lead lives in which they can enjoy the pleasures of sex and love. She could also mean that a certain ideal of beauty or femininity in the globalized context of consumer culture has become a symbol of love and sex, and that Western women symbolically embody the characteristics associated with those ideals.

An alternative or complementary interpretation would be that Chinese women are virtuous while Western women are debauched. A middle-aged editor at an official women's magazine in Beijing believed, in line with such an interpretation, that Western women had sexy and beautiful bodies whereas Chinese women possessed an inner beauty manifested primarily by their politeness (*limao*).[14] This inner beauty, she said, found expression in how Chinese women cared for their homes, husbands, children, and parents. She obviously believes that Western women did not live up to this Chinese ideal. Chinese women were also reserved (*hanxu*), which Western women were not, and Chinese women, she added, strongly disapproved of how outgoing (*pengzhang*) Western women were.

That the Chinese fantasy of the white woman rests on negative stereotypes also comes through in discussions with young female subjects in Beijing and

Guangzhou. The ad for the water heater was deemed to be *tai baolu* (too revealing) or *tai guofende* (going too far). However, other nude or eroticized illustrations of Western women raised no objections. Explicitly erotic or pornographic ads like the ones discussed above do not appear with Chinese models because, as a young Chinese woman explained to me, "Ads with seminude Western women are perfectly acceptable, whereas similar portrayals with Chinese women are not."

Should we then understand these consumerist representations of Western women as examples of a Chinese Occidentalism, a regime of knowledge and desire constructing the West as diametrically opposite, uncivilized, and sexually loose compared to China?[15] In one sense, yes, the Western female body *is* being made into a stereotype of strength, sexuality, and promiscuity that can be consumed without any threat to the traditional virtues of Chinese women. This imaginary simultaneously posits the Occidental Other in a clearly delineated dichotomy of West and East. Ads and interviews portray the white female woman as sexy, passionate, and licentious, in contrast to Chinese women and their inner beauty.[16] This construction mirrors that of a Western Orientalism in which women from the Near East were represented in art and literature as degenerate bearers of primitive passions and sexually available to white male desire.[17] However, this comparison is complicated by the fact that the asymmetric power relations between China and the West have favored the latter. This fact disturbs any reading of Chinese representations of Western women as simply an inversion of Western Orientalism.

Western colonial discourse compared unconquered lands to a woman and called for European explorers to *penetrate virgin* lands and to *unveil* their secrets.[18] This feminization of the non-Western world constructed the people inhabiting Asia and Africa as passive and seductive, while the Western imperial powers imagined themselves as active males, or father figures. In the Chinese ads discussed above, Western women were represented as both strong and sexually active. Asian models were portrayed in subordinate poses. This would indicate not only a reversal of conventional gender roles but also of the position of the Other in colonial discourse. The symbolic position of women in Chinese advertising thus reveals a Chinese masculinization of the Western female Other. This suggests that the eroticized representations of Western women were not limited to heterosexual desire but point to a libidinal economy of race, gender, and power. Chinese minorities in China are certainly the subject of sexual fantasies, but nothing beyond this internal Orientalism disturbs the Chinese identity.[19] The image of the white woman involves something more. As the representation of power and wealth, she becomes a fetish that organizes the social grammar of identity and difference as well as that of desire and fear.

TO HAVE OR NOT HAVE THE SAME SKIN COLOR

In a reading of Orientalism, Homi Bhabha manages to get past moralistically defining representations and stereotypes as simply good or bad. He proposes an alternative interpretation of the racial stereotype that ably encompasses the Chinese context. Referring to what he labels the "Freudian fable of fetishism," Bhabha unpacks the contradictions embedded in Western colonial discourse. By substituting the possession and lack of a penis in gender relations with possession and lack of the same skin color in racial relations, Bhabha reads the racial stereotype as a fetish:

> For fetishism is always a "play" or vacillation between the archaic affirmation of wholeness/similarity — in Freud's terms: "All men have penises"; in ours: "All men have the same skin/race/culture"—and the anxiety associated with lack and difference—again, for Freud: "Some do not have penises"; for us: "Some do not have the same skin/race/culture."[20]

For Freud the fetish was a substitute for the mother's phallus, which the boy once believed in and does not accept the loss of.[21] The fetish functions as a denial of reality, a triumph over and a safeguard against the threat of castration. According to Bhabha, the construction of and the obsession with the Other ultimately springs from primal conceptions of identity and difference. The racial stereotype, like the fetish, is nurtured by a complex of desire, identity, and lack, and gives access to an identity built on mastery and pleasure while simultaneously feeding on anxiety and resistance. This resonates well with the contradicting sets of Chinese images of the West. While the white female is perceived as sexier, the West is still regarded as a moral threat, so in the logic of the fetish, fear and desire must be replaced by mastery and degradation.

In the 1930s a popular author like Lin Yutang could write that Westerners' facial and body hair was proof of the backwardness of their civilization *vis-à-vis* the Chinese, who had lived indoor lives much longer than the Westerners and therefore did not need corporeal hair.[22] Mao Zedong in a moment of Chinese weakness and almost total isolation expressed a similar view. Threatened by the Russians, Mao turned to the archenemy for help. When President Nixon took the decision to visit China, Mao curiously expressed about the Americans, "They are evolving from a monkey into a man, not quite a man yet, the tail is still there."[23]

As historian Frank Dikötter points out, Chinese racial discourse used hairiness to construct bestiality.[24] During Japan's occupation of China, propaganda depicted the Japanese enemy as extremely hairy, and we saw earlier how the

Chinese ideal regarding skin valued hairlessness in contrast with Western women's hairy limbs. Advertising is careful not to use negative images, but in two Chinese ads from 1995 we find images of the West that cater to simian constructions of white people, harking back to the ideas expressed by the likes of Lin Yutang and Mao Zedong revealing a denial of the fear of the Other by turning her into a nonhuman.

In the first ad, a blonde woman stands laughing beside a washing machine that has the word "Revolution" written over it in bold letters.[25] A couple of months later an ad for the same company, Wuxi Little Swan, appears in the same magazine.[26] The blonde woman is replaced by a chimpanzee, made to look human by wearing glasses, a bow tie, a white shirt, and trousers, and with a camera hanging around his neck. The (human) monkey is standing beside the same washing machine with the same word, "Revolution," written over it. And now a logo beside the monkey spells out in childish handwriting, *Wo ye hui yong xiao tiane* (I also can handle Little Swan). Apart from the monkey replacing the white woman, the scene is the same. The monkey not only can handle the washing machine, he can also write Chinese characters, albeit in the clumsy, childish handwriting characteristic of foreigners attempting to come to grips with the written Chinese language. The camera makes the monkey look like a tourist. The effect of dressing up a monkey in clothing is to make him almost human; but with the tourist and foreign connotations of the camera and the poor Chinese handwriting, he is also only *almost* Chinese. The two ads, when read together, clearly advance the notion of Westerners as uncivilized and illustrate the double bind of racial fetishism described by Bhabha.

Contemporaneous with the publication of these ads, the image of a not-quite-human Westerner turned up in other settings that were clearly about fear and its disavowal. For example, in a scene in the extremely popular Chinese soap opera *A Beijing Man in New York*, the protagonist decries Americans to a Chinese friend: "Fuck them! They were still monkeys up in the trees when we were already human beings. Look at how hairy they are, they're not as evolved as we are. Just because they have a bit of money!"[27] The simian association aside, this scene captures the paradox of the West as simultaneously subordinate and powerful in the Chinese imagination, while revealing the desire to dominate this Other, which is also, in an international setting, the big Other of the law and the symbolic order.[28]

These images represent the West as a beastly Other, expressing a Chinese dichotomy of mind and body in which images of white women in Chinese ads reflect the racialized/culturalized idea of sexuality as well as of morality in general. In this racial grammar Western women represent an animalistic sexuality and are ruled by their passions and desires, while Chinese women embody the cultivated virtues of civilization. However, it is not about white women per se but on difference in a more general sense.

CONSUMING WHITE WOMEN

Cultural critic Rey Chow argued in the early 1990s that the white woman had been made a symbol of what China is not or does not have while simultaneously arguing that this white female becomes a fetish that has nothing to do with sex.[29] Chow is right in pointing out that the white woman is imagined as something more than and different from simply the heterosexual opposite of man, but she is perhaps mistaken in claiming that the image of the white woman is not about sex. It is gender categories and sexual fantasies that make up the core logic of the fetish, and, after all, it is the white *woman* who is fetishized. But, that said, it does not necessarily follow that this fetish is a heterosexual construction created to relieve a certain male anxiety. On the contrary, turning to representations involving Chinese men and Western women, we will see that the white woman is not only an object for male sexual desire but also a source of fear that eventually leads to abjection. The racial fetish thus comes to transcend the inherent structure of power relations between men and women, proving that the white fetish is heavily invested in an economy of desire *and* power.

In his elaborate psychological investigation into what it meant to be a black man in a still Western-dominated world, Frantz Fanon in *Black Skin, White Masks* came to the following conclusion regarding what the white woman represented in the racial nexus of postcolonialism:

> But—and this is the form of recognition that Hegel never described—who better than the white woman to bring this about? By loving me, she proves that I am worthy of a white love. I am loved like a white man. I am a white man.[30]

Is it something similar the white woman represents for the Chinese: recognition from the West? The widely discussed television series *A Beijing Man in New York*, referred to previously, describes the hardships of a Chinese couple who emigrates from Beijing to the Western metropolis of New York. The male Chinese protagonist has to give up his career as a musician in an elite symphony orchestra and take employment washing dishes in a Chinese restaurant. He not only loses his former profession but also his social position, suffering humiliation at the very bottom of American society. When the Chinese immigrant eventually manages to work himself up from poverty, he picks up a white, blonde, buxom prostitute on whom to vent his pent-up frustrations. During intercourse, he showers the white woman with dollar bills, demanding that she cry out repeatedly, "I love you."[31]

The sinologist Geremie Barmé uses this scene to initiate a discussion about resurgent nationalism among Chinese intellectuals. According to Barmé, the scene was extremely popular with the Chinese audience in Mainland China. He describes how an émigré Chinese had exclaimed about the show that "to screw foreign cunt is a kind of patriotism" (*cai waiguo bi ye suan aiguo ma*).[32] To buy and to consume a white, blonde, blue-eyed American for these individuals was metaphoric Chinese revenge for a century of Western imperialism. It also illustrated China's new-felt economic power in the world.[33] But as we shall see, this phantasm, rather than being triumphal, is actually about anxiety, insecurity, and fear.

The scene from *A Beijing Man in New York* parallels an earlier work, the beloved Zhang Ailing [Eileen Chang] novel *Hong meigui yu bai meigui* (*Red Rose, White Rose*), in which a similar amorous encounter plays out between a Chinese student in Europe and a blonde, blue-eyed prostitute in Paris with whom he loses his virginity.[34] After returning from his studies abroad, he brags about this episode to his male Chinese friends, saying, "Before I got to Paris, I was only a boy." The memory of the incident, however, resists his conscious effort to transform it into a romantic and endearing affair. Instead it leaves him disgusted. That warm summer's eve in Paris, as he describes it to himself, he was out for a stroll when he suddenly encountered a French prostitute, who takes him to a nearby hostel and seduces him.[35] The Chinese protagonist remembers secretly watching the woman anxiously raise her arm and sniff her armpit. What turned him off, however, was not so much her body odor as her insecurity, he recalls. Considering the situation—he a virgin and she a prostitute—this episode actually reads like a projection of the student's own anxieties. And, in fact, he laments that he could not control even a woman like her. "He spent money on her body but still couldn't become her master" (*ta zai ta shenshang huale qian, ye hai zuobuliao tade zhuren*), the narrator tells us.

After coitus her appearance suddenly takes on masculine traits. "It was the gloomy, cold face of a man, the face of an ancient warrior," the former student tells his friends.[36] The scene he wants to recollect as the moment he attains his manhood was a terrifying experience during which the racial fetish turns back on him with full power. Instead of him becoming a man, as he bragged to his friends, it is the white woman who turns into a potent male warrior. Read this in contrast to the intertext of *M. Butterfly*, discussed above, in which a Chinese man dresses as a woman. Here in Chang's novel, a real, Western woman suddenly appears to be a man.

Returning to *A Beijing Man in New York*, Barmé interprets the Chinese émigré and the American prostitute in New York as representing "the coming of age of Chinese narcissism," bespeaking "a desire for revenge for all the real and perceived slights of the past century."[37] The Chinese émigré's wish for the prostitute to cry out, "I love you," not only is a perfect *mise-en-scène* of the Lacanian impossibility of fulfilling desire, it also captures the trope of the fetish. It is about that which he cannot get from her because she does not have it. He not only wants the white prostitute sexually, he wants her love and recognition, which he knows she is not selling.

In the book on which the screenplay is based, this scene plays out differently and is more in line with Zhang Ailing's story. The frustration of the man is replaced by impotence, and his own subjugation substitutes for his command of the woman. In the book, the Beijing man in New York ventures by chance into a porn movie theater.[38] He is approached by a prostitute who entices him into a secluded booth, where she makes him sit and proceeds to give him a blow job. When he remains unaroused, the prostitute asks him if he is chicken, slaps his butt, and demands that he pay up. He stumbles out and, the book continues, ". . . he never dared to roam astray again." In Zhang Ailing's story, the man wants to possess and control the white prostitute. "He spent money on her body," that is, on sex, but what he really coveted was control and power. After failing he decides to create a right (*dui*) world for himself, and in "this miniature world he would always be the definitive master." Just like the Beijing Man, the protagonist of the *Red Rose, White Rose*'s fear of impotence leads to abjection.

The reaction of the men in these two stories when they get too close to their desired object resembles what Slavoj Žižek writes about the gaze:

> The fetish object *par excellence* (nothing fascinates me more than the Other's gaze, which is fascinated in so far as it perceives that which is "in me more than myself," the secret treasure at the kernel of my being), but it can also shift into the harbinger of the horror of castration (the gaze of Medusa's head).[39]

Both men are seduced by the fetishized white woman. But she actively takes control of the situation and at the moment of fulfillment of their racialized sexual fantasies, the men are struck by Medusa's gaze and flee their imminent castration.

To conclude, free, licentious sex is invested into the image of Western women, articulating with disturbing effectiveness the fetishist mode of the stereotype: the desire for power and domination over the Other, a desire that ultimately grows out of fear. Read together, the three scenes discussed above express an almost identical psychological investment in the trope of the white woman. Besides describing the psychology of race, sex, and power on a personal level, these scenes could also be read together as a postcolonial allegory on wanting what the West has—a fetish represented as the white woman.

MEDUSA'S HEAD

There was obviously more to the representations of Western women in Chinese advertising from the 1990s than a simple reference to the West. That the advertisements display Western women as powerful and attractive indicates that Chinese women in the specific gender politics of the 1990s were still perceived as precluded from an imagined femininity that entailed *both* power *and* pleasure. These characteristics are instead projected onto Western women, who are presented as having what Chinese women lack. While Western women are portrayed as powerful, self-satisfied, sexually attractive, and equal with men, Asian women are represented as children. This contrast resembles constructions of gender relations in Western ads but with the important difference that in Chinese ads, the white woman occupies the position that men characteristically have in Western ads. It is as if these women symbolically possess what Freud claimed women could not possess, and the symbolic space of the West is thus effectively masculinized.

In the logic of the fetish, the promise of pleasure coexists with a wish for power as the white female body is inscribed in a larger geopolitical and historical context of Chinese-Western relations. She appears not only in a Chinese fantasy of pleasure, but also in a libidinal economy of domination and power. These images we have been analyzing express a threat, not only to Chinese self-identity, but also to China's aspirations to become a modern, strong, rich, and potent nation. The gaze of the Western Other, who perceives "in me more than myself," is also always intrinsically dangerous. It can turn into the castrating gaze of Medusa's head. This, read together with the substitution of gender with race, makes the white woman in Chinese advertising and popular culture resemble the *racial* fetishism Bhabha posits. In the global flows of culture, positive images of the West disturb assumptions of a shared Chinese cultural identity. The image of the Western Other therefore not only represents a promise, but also poses a threat to the idea of a full identity. Lacan describes the fullness of the stereotype— its image as its identity—as always being threatened by incompleteness. This is what is expressed in the Chinese's fetishized stereotype of the West: a desire to have what the Other has, plus an aggressive reaction to the fear of Western containment that reads like a fear of castration.

We have in this longer chapter already taken a first step in such a direction, so let us now end this study with moving from the inside of a Chinese gender discourse—as seen from the developing consumer culture of the 1990s—to the global circulation of sexualized fantasies about the Other and the Self, namely to the libidinal economy of "China."

NOTES

1. Žižek 1997, 104.
2. Mulvey 1975, 6–18.
3. The following reading of Chinese ads featuring Caucasian-looking women is limited to ads produced solely for use in China. Ads originally created for another national, regional, or global audience are excluded. The selection consists of all ads that appeared from 1990 to 1995 in *Zhiyin* (*Bosom Friend*), *Hunyin yu jiating* (*Marriage and Family*), *Shaonü* (*Teenage Girl*), *Zhongguo funü* (*Chinese Women*), *Fenyou* (*Share the Burden*), and *Nüyou* (*Women's Friend*). These magazines were all published and edited by the All-China Women's Federation, and range from more serious magazines directed toward middle-aged women to popular publications that targeted young women and teenage girls.
4. Goffman 1987, 24.
5. Ibid., 40.
6. *Zhiyin* (*Bosom Friend*) (121), January 1995, 65.
7. *Hunyin yu jiating* (*Marriage and Family*), June 1990.
8. Brownell 1996, 237.
9. *Hunyin yu jiating* (*Marriage and Family*), July 1995.
10. McClintock 1995, 181–203.
11. *Fenyou* (*Share the Burden*), September 1994. A similar ad had appeared a couple of months earlier; it showed a blonde woman in a damp top with water streaming down from a shower onto her breasts.
12. *Shaonü* (*Teenage Girl*), 1993, the back page. The ad was for a body-lengthening device.
13. Interview in Canton, April 1996.
14. Interview in Beijing, April 1996.
15. Although this is not the place to go deeper into various descriptions of Occidentalism, it is necessary to mention two opposing understandings of this discourse on the West. First we have that of Margalit and Buruma, finding a tradition going way back to a romanticist critique of enlightenment and then cherished by the Communists as well as the Islamist enemies of the West. An opposing viewpoint, skeptical to both the vilifying of the West and the binary of East and West or the West and the Rest is found in Chen Xiaomei's text on Chinese Occidentalism. In a number of examples from the fields of culture and politics, she argues for a more fluid relationship between the West and its Others.
16. Resembling what Gerth (2003) recounted in the discourse of the 1930s on "authentic" vs "false" Chinese women, depending on if they followed Western fashion and bought imported cosmetics or not.
17. Said 1985, 190.
18. See McClintock 1995, 24–25.
19. The Other of Chinese colonial discourse exists instead in stereotypes of dark-skinned people from Africa and Southeast Asia and "minority people." Anthropologist Louisa Schein has described this Chinese discourse on minority people as an "internal Orientalism" (see Louisa Schein's 1997 article).
20. Bhabha 1994, 74.
21. See Freud's article "Fetishism" in the standard edition, vol. 7.
22. Lin Yutang 1935, 27.
23. See MacMillan 2008, 196.

24. Dikötter 1992, 141.
25. *Zhongguo funü* (*Chinese women*), March 1995.
26. *Zhongguo funü* (*Chinese women*), October 1995.
27. Quoted from Barmé 1995, 210 n. 2.
28. Just as an example, see how international relations specialist John Ikenberry (2013) discusses the threat of China's rise to the United States, arguing that it is the whole liberal international order—the only one we have—that China is up against and that it is actually impossible to challenge that system. Standing outside the law, the social, or the international order threatens the very survival of the individual, or of the state.
29. Chow 1991, 86.
30. Fanon 1967, 45.
31. Barmé 1995, 209. It is worth also mentioning the TV soap opera *Foreign Babes in Beijing*, which became so popular it was in short time rebroadcast five times. Here Western women are similarly portrayed as highly active sexually, taking initiatives and managing to rob feebler Chinese women of their husbands.
32. Ibid. The joke is formed by the fact that the literal translation of *aiguo* or "patriotism" is *love-nation* and *aiguo* rhymes with *waiguo*, which is Chinese for "foreign."
33. Ibid., 210.
34. Zhang Ailing 1996.
35. Ibid., 25.
36. Ibid., 26.
37. Barmé 1995, 210.
38. Cao Guilin 1991, 77.
39. Žižek 1997, 104. He is here following Part Two of Lacan's *The Four Fundamental Concepts of Psychoanalysis*.

Chapter Six

The Sexual Geopolitics of "China"

This study has so far linked nationalist sentiments to a Chinese discourse on gender, desire, and need for recognition. In Hegelian phenomenology, a subject must be recognized by another to properly exist. The People's Republic of China coming into being in the heat of the Cold War was denied that recognition from the international community.[1] All this has changed and China is becoming incorporated into the global state of affairs. But what is the nature of China's foreign relations today as it moves toward its old dream of wealth, power, recognition, and respect? How does the Hegelian idea that each human being is in the being of the Other translate into international relations, and, the main point of this study, what role do desire, femininity, and power play in such an identity construction?

In this concluding chapter we will take a step away from the above discussion on the corporeal politics, the bodily metaphor, and gender discourse to discuss more directly not China's libidinal economy, but the libidinal economy of "China." Our focus shifts from analyzing how woman is employed in a Chinese nationalist discourse to how China is articulated in a sexual geopolitics. In a hermeneutical bow we return to the broader context where we first situated the cultural dimension of a Chinese body politics in the Introduction. We now ask what China represents in the gaze of the West, how China is imagined as a counterpart of a mainly American geopolitical project, and how the symmetry of "racial castration" and "white fetishism" plays out in a Chinese reply to this American phantasm.

CULTURE AND POWER

The first best-selling Chinese book of this millennium was a more than 400-pages-long autobiographical novel about wolves, manhood, and history.

With half a million copies sold during the six months after its release in 2004, *Lang Tuteng* (*Wolf Totem*) was not only an instant blockbuster, it also caused a heated debate on politics and national character.[2] Judging from its content, this seems quite odd at first. *Lang Tuteng* tells the story of three young men from Beijing who are sent to work in Inner Mongolia during the Cultural Revolution. Taking part in everyday chores as a horse- and sheep-raising nomad, the narrator and his friends develop an interest in wolves, which springs from the adoption of a wolf cub and taking on the role of its substitute mother. This interest soon turns into an obsession.[3] Besides describing life among the Mongols, *Lang Tuteng* carries an important subtext on the importance of the wolf for both nomadic and settled populations throughout China's history. The argument is that the Chinese have become a people of sheep and need to relearn the way of the wolf, not only for their personal satisfaction but for China to become a competitive nation in the aggressive domain of international relations. According to the Chinese boys in the story, wolves, like nomads, are natural warriors.

Despite its somewhat odd subject, it should not have surprised anyone even slightly familiar with *fin-de-siècle* China that *Lang Tuteng* became an instant best-seller. Beginning in the mid-1990s, as we have seen, a stream of nationalistic diatribes appeared, more aggressive in nationalist assertiveness than before but still anxious about China's abilities and future. For Western observers these texts represented an intimidating discourse and therefore became the focus of much attention. Since the resurgent Chinese nationalism of the 1990s was emotional, enigmatic, and seemingly difficult to control, Peter Hays Gries, an American expert on Sino-American relations, advised a psychological approach to explain the dynamics of what he labeled "China's new nationalism."[4] This was a fresh and productive perspective. But while Hays Gries's analysis used the concept of "face" for finding a way out of American-Chinese misunderstandings, here we will take another path, using a psychoanalytical framework. A path that accepts the dialectics of this relationship, not just seeing how one suffers and the other is to blame, but how both reinforce each other's identities and the construction of a shared geopolitical complex on desire, disappointment, and aggression.

The subject of our investigation is the dialectics of nationalism and identity building, and our objective is to untangle the web of desire and sexual identification that exists between China and the West. To paraphrase Fredric Jameson, we will try to establish a geopolitical unconscious in popular culture. The basic understanding is that national identity-building cannot be isolated to any internal discourse, so we will first investigate how China is represented and imagined in Hollywood fantasies *and* in Chinese nationalistic literature. A discussion about *Lang Tuteng* is both the starting point and the conclusion of the chapter.

Instead of seeing the dialectics of identity construction as producing misconception requiring resolution, as Hays Gries does, the following discussion adheres to the notion that fantasies about the intentions of the Other also bring a collective together. Fantasy is simultaneously the only mode we have to recognize others *and* our main support for sex and—more generally—desire. Jacques Lacan explained that the original question of desire was not, "What do I want?" but "What do others want from me?"[5] This is the main realization of our examining China's fantasy about East and West—that also revolves around the questions: What do they see in me? What am I to others? The assumption is that Chinese identity construction is essentially a fantasy connected to the perceived desire of the West (what that Other sees in China), which fuels also the workings of the desire and aggression of China's new nationalism.

MELANCHOLIA—OR WHY THE WEST LOST CHINA

For much of the period the CCP describes as a "hundred years of humiliation," the United States imagined itself to possess a "special relationship" with China.[6] This had to do first and foremost with the American missionaries and the idea of the United States not being one of the "old" imperialist nations of the West. Later, during World War II, it was the shared destiny of fighting the Japanese coupled with the American dream of a postwar world ruled by the United States together with a Christian, liberal, and democratic China under Chiang Kai-shek. Finally, after America's self-perceived "loss of China" a new economic union has been forged in what has even been at one time called "Chimerica." But it is the period in between, that of the Cold War, to which we will turn first, a period when, as Christine Klein argues, the Americans "turned their attention eastward" while churning out a multitude of cultural texts with East Asia and the Pacific as the subject matter.[7] But there is also a gendered aspect to add to Klein's "Cold War Orientalism" as we will see in the following.

Also dealing with America's relation to East Asia, Gina Marchetti in her book, *Romance and the "Yellow Peril,"* shows how Hollywood effectively solves geopolitical contradictions in a mythical manner. Discussing two films from the 1950s—*Love Is a Many-Splendored Thing* and *The World of Suzy Wong*, she demonstrates how Hollywood reaffirms an American masculinity that was threatened by the entry of women into traditionally male workplaces during World War II. The films achieve this reaffirmation, she writes, by telling stories of Caucasian men saving Chinese women. In *The World of Suzy Wong*, for example, an American painter played by William Holden rescues the prostitute Suzy Wong (played by Nancy Kwan) from the slums of Hong

Kong. Marchetti directs our attention here to the idea of "the white knight": the male hero whom generations of Western girls believed would transport them to a beautiful life—a fantasy that situates women as passive, waiting for salvation by their Prince Charming.[8]

There is, however, more to these Hollywood films about China. If one plays down the omnipotence of the male gaze and considers instead the seductive quality of the female object's withdrawal from and resistance to the white man's attempts to save her, then an additional story appears. Marchetti herself at one point notes how the female protagonists waver, initially seeming to not be interested in salvation at all. In *Love Is a Many-Splendored Thing*, a film based on a Han Suyin story, the female lead opts to leave everything she has—including her Western lover—to help out as a doctor in a China where the Communists have just taken power.[9] This is clearly a feminine sacrifice, but Marchetti does not attempt to explain *why* the woman makes the sacrifice.

A film that does not take place in Hong Kong but inside China in the tumultuous, radical, and transformative year of 1926 does offer a context in which to better understand this mysterious withdrawal of women. *The Sand Pebbles* features Steve McQueen as a machinist on an American gunboat patrolling the Yangtze River. The story takes place during a time of strong nationalist sentiments when, aided by the Soviet Union, Chiang Kai-shek leads a Chinese army to reunite a nation divided among warlords. As has been true during other periods of Chinese nationalistic upheaval, popular feelings turned strongly xenophobic, making it dangerous for Westerners living in the cities located upriver on the Yangtze. Despite this tension between China and the West, the important subplot of this film is about an American crewman falling in love with and then attempting to rescue a depressed young Chinese woman. When he gets to know the secret behind her sadness (that she is a prostitute), he promises to buy her freedom from the brothel where she is forced to work.

While this liberation of a woman is taking place, Steve McQueen's character is teaching English to a Chinese boatman, as well as helping him master the ship engine. The engine is a synecdoche for Western technology and is treated with superstition and fear by the other Chinese boatmen. An obvious struggle for the Chinese soul is going on here, and halfway into the film the Chinese environment turns hostile toward the Americans. By then, the American sailor has purchased the Chinese prostitute's freedom and married her. But, mysteriously, she is more depressed than ever, has stopped speaking, and is turning frailer by the minute. She is pining for her former life, we learn, and wants to return to her tormentors.

In *The Sand Pebbles*, unlike in Marchetti's examples, the subject matter is not so much about American masculinity as it is about the Chinese backdrop. The prostitute serves allegorically for a China in which Americans had invested so much money and energy to save it from the Japanese but that, in the end, they lost to Communism. This *loss of China* was traumatic for many Americans, who asked why the Chinese did not want to be saved the same way as Western Europe.[10] Why did China withdraw from the outstretched hand, and why did it revert to isolationism?

Film critic Michel Chion offers a radical model of cause and effect that could shed light on if not China's withdrawal into Maoist ideology, then at least on the American sense of loss and disbelief. Chion argues in his book on the filmmaker David Lynch that the connection between cause and effect is akin to the sexual relation between men and women.[11] His analog question becomes, "Can female enjoyment be reduced to an effect of what the man does with her?"[12] In his view it is the woman who breaks the chain of cause and effect, and it is female depression that causes this collapse of causality. How does one deal with the female subject's dangerous retreat into herself, her depressive nonalignment with the world? The men in David Lynch's movies, as Chion explains, assault the depressed woman, attempting to shock or frighten her out of her lethargy.

We find an example of both the syndrome Chion lays out and its cure in a more recent film in which battered Western masculinity is absolved by a woman standing in for China. In fact, the salvation of a depressed woman seems to be exactly what Michael Cimino's 1985 film, *Year of the Dragon*, is about. Just as in the 1950s' *The Sand Pebbles*, Cimino's story is easily recognized as a sexual allegory about China and the West.[13]

Mickey Rourke plays a cop named Stanley White, who wages war against opium syndicates in New York's Chinatown. White's ambition is to save this *Little China* by doing away with the corrupt and violent Chinese individuals who run it. He makes a great effort to learn about all things Chinese, even enlisting a Chinese-American policeman to assist him. Opposing White is Chinese-American television newscaster Tracy Tsu (played by Ariane Koizumi). From her first appearance in the film, she looks unhappy, acting jaded and standoffish.

His pursuit for allies, his eagerness to learn more about Chinatown, and his loneliness as an outsider lead White to woo Tsu. He invites her to a posh Chinese restaurant, bringing with him the book *Things Chinese* to show his knowledge and resolve to the young woman. As they quietly dine and chat, members from two warring triads suddenly storm into the restaurant, firing their weapons in all directions. White saves the screaming Tsu from the flying bullets by violently throwing himself on top of her body, thus clearly spelling out the nature of their relationship.

In a subsequent scene White tries to pick up Tsu. Irritated she brushes him off, saying, "I'm no Saigon hooker, am I?" But she jumps in his car anyway and they drive to her place. At Tsu's apartment, White, who also is a

Vietnam War veteran, explains he hates her for being Asian and for being on television, and then tells her he is horny. Police officer White then takes the young Chinese-American woman by force right there on the floor, despite her struggle and protests. After this violent act and without asking her permission, White moves into her flat, bringing with him all his books about China.

Officer White's shockingly irregular, aggressive behavior puts Tsu off balance; strangely, it also provokes her and alarms her into her first smile in the film. White makes her laugh and after making love, Tsu suddenly tells this rapist cop that she loves him. The attack, assault, and rape by this Caucasian-American male policeman provoke the Chinese-American woman (in the same way it provokes all of *Little China*) out of depression. The *white* officer awakens the *Chinese* woman with something that could best be described as shock therapy, and despite his treatment of her as a Saigon hooker she loves him. When the White Knight saves Tsu and wins her over with violent sex, can it take long before he also crushes the evil of *Little China*?

With lion dances, opium lairs, and gambling dens, *Year of the Dragon* presents a sort of eternal, mythical Chinatown. Remarkable in this postmodern pastiche is White's obsessive interest in "things Chinese." It is, he seems to believe, his knowledge of China that will save Chinatown. He is therefore always prepared to learn more, if not from books, then from his Chinese informants. In his ethnographic interest in New York's Chinatown, White clearly resembles the Orientalists of the previous century, that is, the Western scholar described in Edward Said's seminal text, who also believed his knowledge about the Asian Other would save Asian peoples and cultures from ruin.[14] Just what was the Asian predicament, according to these Western Orientalists? Well, for the Occidental imperialists, Asia was in a lethargic state and needed to be awakened from its age-old slumber. After he conquered Egypt, Napoleon referred to China as a sleeping lion;[15] the Orientalists viewed waking the Orient from its introspective condition of imagined self-sufficiency as a kind of salvation.[16] In order to start a modernization process afresh, the Orient needed to be shocked out of its melancholia, which one can argue had been caused by its inability to properly mourn the loss of civilization and bygone glory. It fell upon heroic white knights like Lawrence of Arabia to combine knowledge and love of the Orient with an energetic and sometimes brutal disposition to craft this awakening and change. This was once also the most widely influential Western interpretation of the modernization of China, as epitomized in the Fairbank interpretation of Chinese history, dominant for so many decades, which held that it was stimuli coming from the West that forced China into adopting modernizing reforms.[17]

This is, of course, all fantasy. However, the American obsession with China and its sticking to an idea of a "special relationship" between the United States and China, even if it has to be forced upon the latter, has throughout history caused a very problematic, tense situation in the Chinese reaction to this American demand.

HYSTERIA—OR THE QUESTION OF CHINA'S NEW NATIONALISM

Napoleon's metaphor of China as the sleeping lion was soon replaced with the notion of China being the invalid of Asia. The mighty Ottoman Empire had also been "sick" and had simply disappeared after World War I when Western imperialist powers divided it up. The idea of social Darwinism led early twentieth-century Chinese students and intellectuals to feel an acute threat of national dismemberment or even erasure. This sense of crisis brought about the decline of traditional Chinese ways and the introduction of a rejuvenated May Fourth culture. It was, we should remember, the goal of rousing as many souls as possible up from their coma that led one of those intellectuals, Lu Xun, to become a writer and compile the stories in his debut work, *Call to Arms* (*Na han*).

Since the reform attempts of the late nineteenth century, Chinese intellectuals, writers, and artists have equated their lives, careers, and works with the fortunes of the nation. This conflation is readily seen in Yu Dafu's widely read novel *Sinking*, a story about a Chinese student in Japan who blames his lack of self-esteem and his inability to approach women on the poor state of his motherland. That theme made *Sinking* a Chinese best-seller and heralded an ever-growing fixation on the fate of the nation and of being Chinese.[18] The angst caused by conflating the Self with the dire state of the nation, coupled with the inability to disengage from the national object so characteristic of twentieth-century Chinese intellectuals, artists, and authors led C. T. Hsia, in his acclaimed history of Chinese literature, to talk about "the obsession with China."[19] Zhong Xueping, in a feminist reading of Chinese literature from the 1980s, takes Hsia's insight a step further, pointing out how, when the sentiments of the May Fourth era resurfaced, Chinese intellectuals came under a "male marginality complex," seeing themselves as feminized in their relations toward the Chinese state.[20] In her interpretation this all goes back to the reactions of the Confucian officials-intellectuals, whose sense of masculinity stemmed from their being the sage upholders of a universal empire. When challenged by Western imperialism and wholly alien intellectual ideals, this masculinity was laid under "siege."

A related phenomenon to Hsia's obsession with China and the "siege" mentality described by Zhong Xueping is the so-called "Nobel complex"—the anger and anxiety for China caused by the absence of any Nobel Prize.[21] Literary critic Zhang Xudong explains this Nobel complex as being about a desire to be recognized by the Western Other.[22] In such a worldview, every comment about China that the West makes is amplified into a roaring judgment that either accepts or rejects, he argues.[23] This obsession with China paradoxically focuses both on *recognition* from as well as *rejection* by the West.

This paranoiac demand from the Other is the constant companion of a Chinese desire for self-reliance. Although Mao Zedong managed to "liberate" China, the symbolic importance of the West remained strong. This was apparent not just because all the propaganda on how antirevolutionary, bourgeois, or simply *foreign* threats hindered the construction of a modern China, but it also impeded the desire to catch up with and become just like its adversary, the West.[24]

The 1980s, a decade of openness and infatuation with the West, came to an end with the Tiananmen Square massacre. The massive international criticism directed against the PRC's brutal ways of managing social protest helped produce a renewed Chinese mistrust of the intentions of the alien Other and led China to withdraw inward again. The so-called new Chinese nationalism of the 1990s found it perfectly sensible to interpret the West's behavior in sinister terms. But the bloody crackdown in 1989 also spelled the definitive end of communism in China. In what had suddenly become a postsocialist world, the CCP, as we have seen, launched "love-the-country-ism" to reconnect the Chinese people with the Communist Party.

China's new nationalism played out throughout the 1990s in a number of incidents. Among the more violent manifestations was, as referred to above, the outburst after the American bombing of the Chinese embassy in Belgrade, perceived by the public—with tacit support from the authorities—as an intentional insult, and angry Chinese student protestors demanded blood revenge. Nationalism was intensified also by events such as China's not being selected to host the 2000 Olympic Games, which was blamed on the West not granting China this coming-out opportunity. A popular book written by Chinese intellectuals and students who had spent time in the United States, as we have seen, concluded that Western media were demonizing China.[25]

The Chinese intellectuals' infatuation with the West of the 1980s turned 180 degrees in the 1990s. Interest in theory and scholarship coming from Western academia was now reworked into serving a China-centered agenda. Official Chinese nationalism merged with postcolonial theories to create an essentially anti-Western and Sino-centric discourse, thus managing to fortify already strong ideas about Chinese victimization and adding new fuel to the belief of a "Century of humiliation" (*bainian guochi*).[26] Peter Hays Gries explains in his long essay on Chinese new nationalism how the image of China as a raped woman, prevalent in Republican times but unpopular in the self-asserting Maoist period, now reemerged.[27] What was the logic behind the comeback of this sexual trope and how did it relate to the frenzied outburst of *fin-de-siècle* popular nationalism?

Thinking metaphorically about international relations and national identity lets us approach the Chinese new nationalism from the 1990s forward as a hysterical symptom; not as just a socio-psychological diagnosis but rather with the symbolic world order in mind.

The feminist critic Hélène Cixous comments on that most famous Freudian neurotic case, saying that the hysteria of the woman "Dora" is in fact a complaint about the "elementary structures of kinship" against the family pattern of nineteenth century bourgeoisie patriarchy where women were exchanged as objects between families. In an interview Cixous explains, "Dora seemed to me to be the one who resists the system, the one who cannot stand that the family and society are founded on the body of women."[28] In this reading the hysterical symptoms of Dora form a refusal against being abused. Dora rejects the dominant modes of identification and shows she does not want to take her expected place in the symbolic universe of her time.

Transplanted to the Chinese body of nationalist outbursts described above, this reading highlights feelings of injustices of a postcolonial hegemonic ideology that still privileges the former imperialists. And when the nationalist protesting diatribe, *Zhongguo keyi shuo bu* (*China Can Say No*), hit the market in 1996, as we described above, it accordingly generated much concern in the West. A group of established Chinese intellectuals there screamed out against a geopolitical system they felt subordinated and contained China. It was time to say "No!" to the United States, they argued. This outcry of refusal to play along in the power structure of international relations fed right into a passionate popular nationalism transmuting into demonstrations all over China.

With the new American world order following the collapse of the Soviet Union, it was maybe not much of a surprise that Chinese intellectuals, just like Dora, wanted to cry out "No!" to a position assigned to them by the big Other of the international system. But being a bodily symptom of some traumatic experience in the past, what does the hysteric really say through neurosis? According to Jacques Lacan, hysteria consists of the question: "What is it to be a woman?"[29] Lacan focuses here on the ego of identification and its relation to the subject. Turning to Freud's case about the young woman Dora, Lacan then directs us to the surprising place where we find the ego of this hysteric.[30] Dora has symptoms that Freud traces back through a sexual invitation from a Herr K., whose wife Dora's father is courting and with whom Dora is flirting in order to put herself in the position of her father's love object, Herr K.'s wife. Lacan argues that Herr K. is where Dora's ego is located. He refers to the mirror stage and the role of the image in that scheme: "where the subject situates his sense as to recognize himself."[31]

For Freud, a girl's road through the Oedipus complex is longer but initially goes down the same path of love and identification as does a boy's. Initially there is only one gender—a daughter identifies with the father just like a son does. Therefore, Lacan argues, one of the genders, namely the female, is required to take the image of the *other* gender as the basis for identification, not because of the lack of a biological phallus, but because of the symbolic value of lack.[32] The sexual symbolization that takes place requires a virilization of men and that the woman truly accept her feminine function. The hysteric's question is therefore a symptom telling us that the sexual symbolization is not successful. "Becoming a woman and wondering what a woman is, are two essentially different things," Lacan clarifies.[33] When Dora is brooding about "what is a woman," Lacan argues she is symbolizing the female gender as such, that is, the lack of phallus.

So what if we were to understand the new Chinese nationalism as a symptom of the body national, signaling exactly such a rejection of geopolitical symbolization? After all, one of the chapters in *Zhongguo keyi shuo bu (China Can Say No)* was titled, "Take your dirty hands off; we don't want any sexual harassment."

A conclusion like this must also redirect our understanding of the populist diatribes discussed above. We should of course suspect that the nationalist discourse is not so much about the misdoings of the Western Other as it is about the symbolic position of China. The final task of this chapter will proceed from this conclusion, namely, linking the hysteric's question to the melancholic's withdrawal into herself in order to detect a Chinese overinvestment in history.

FROM LITTLE LAMB TO WOLF MAN

It was when Freud struggled to cure one of his most famous patients, the "Wolf Man," that he made the revolutionary realization about the importance of personal history for a patient's neurotic disease. From this discovery arose the insistence of psychoanalysis to focus not only on excavating traumas but also on reworking a patient's life history as a healing method. As Hegel pointed out, history is *nachträglich*, or retroactive, and it is only in retrospect and with contemporary frames of reference that we understand the past (or rather, create a historic narrative).[34] This Freudian method for treatment also moves in the opposite direction, retroactively rewriting history in light of a new present: what is repressed is made conscious, and the disturbing symptoms disappear.

History is in the last instance not about positivist fact-seeking but about creating meaning. History is an account as much from the perspective of the present as it is an attempt to be true to the realities of the times it analyzes. This *mythic* dimension of history corresponds to how psychoanalysis regards working with a patient's past. The proper dimension of psychoanalysis is therefore not that of Reality but of Truth.[35] Freud's famous case of the Wolf Man illustrates well the psychological tension between reality and truth.

The curious name Wolf Man was given to a Russian patient after he revealed a haunting recurring nightmare to Freud.[36] In it the window to his room swings open, revealing a group of white wolves sitting quietly in a tree and *looking* at him. Freud's patient associates this dream with a book illustration of a wolf standing upright on its two hind legs like a human being, an image that terrified him as a child. In his unsuccessful attempt to treat this patient, Freud focused on what he deduced must have been a repressed memory in which, as a baby, the Wolf Man watched his parents having sex. For Freud the wolf represents the patient's father engaged in an amorous situation with the mother. In this reenactment of the Oedipal complex, the boy fears that the father will castrate him for wanting to make love with his mother.[37]

Freud gets to this conclusion by reversing the image of the wolf, holding that the image of six or seven white wolves sitting in a tree comes from a fairy tale in which a wolf kills and eats seven young goats (kids).[38] The Wolf Man eventually remembers the sheep near the manor where he lived as a child. A disease had broken out and the sheep died in droves—certainly a disturbing image for a young boy. So in the dream, the wolves in the tree are not really wolves but young lambs (kids), and the Wolf Man puts himself in the position of a lamb by letting this image conflate with that of the wolves. Similarly the illustration of the wolf standing upright—used by his sister to scare him—also places this Russian neurotic in a position of passive victim as a little lamb about to be devoured.

Freud concludes that the upright-standing wolf that the boy fears is an image of the father. But counter to that reading and borne out by the boy's later development together with a sexual/aggressive encounter he has with a young housemaid, we could argue the boy identifies this role with delight as well as fear.[39] Is that not also the role of the father in the Oedipal drama? Does he not represent for the boy the fearful threat of castration that is simultaneously the point of identification, that is, the euphoric position of *jouissance*?

A dialectic of identification similar to what is going on in the unconscious of the Wolf Man is found in *Lang Tuteng*. While the lamb is a Western symbol of erotic innocence, the Chinese *selang* (sex wolf) is a lecher. In *Lang Tuteng*, the wolf is associated not only with manliness and strength, but also with promiscuous, aggressive sexuality. The author of the book believes that through the centuries, all these attributes have gone missing in China. Although the young Chinese protagonists do not have much of a romantic life during their years in Inner Mongolia, an explicit connection is nevertheless made among sexuality, animals, and ethnicity. After a couple of years on the steppe, the boys feel stronger and more virile. But they are still ridiculed for being weak Chinese "sheep."

With much of the book being about masculinity and male bonding, having a wolf totem equates with being tough, cunning, and savage.[40] This becomes a story about three book-loving, soft, passive city boys trying to take on a more masculine identity. When women do appear in the story, they are threatening. In one scene, a Mongol woman jokingly questions the virility of one of the three students. In another a drunken Mongol man asks when it will be time for the young Chinese men to have sex with a Mongol woman, only to then warn them that Mongolian women are as ferocious as wolves when one gets under the skin rug with them.[41]

The subtext of the book, as should be clear by now, is about Chinese identity. "Mongols are wolves, Chinese are sheep," is the repeated message in *Lang Tuteng*. In this sense the text is not only about how to become more of a wolf, but also what it is to *not* be a wolf and what it means to be a sheep or a lamb.

This zoological metaphor was not an unprecedented feature in a best-seller about Chinese identity. It actually appeared quite frequently in the nationalist discourse of the 1990s. In narratives on China's history, Western nations and Japan, for example, were described as wolves.[42] China, on the other hand, was the victim, threatened by these avaricious wolves, "as weak as lambs at the slaughterhouse."[43] Traditionally in China the lamb is a symbol of filial piety: it goes down on its knees when it sucks its mother's teat. But in the nationalistic texts of the 1990s, it is the Christian symbolism of the lamb that is being employed. The lamb stands for the victim, in the way that Jesus Christ, the Lamb of God, was sacrificed. *Lang Tuteng* is not primarily about the wolf-like character of the Mongols because in the Chinese dichotomy of Self and Other, the West is still both the main adversary *and* the Ideal Ego. The argument is that somewhere back in history, there was a common ground but, as the author explains, "The West took the path of a 'wolf civilization' and the Chinese (*huaxia*) became a 'sheep civilization.'"[44]

This dichotomy in *Lang Tuteng* between Self and Other is, as we have seen, typical of a century of Chinese soul searching. The widely discussed television series that aired in 1988, *Heshang* (*River Elegy*), told a similar story, depicting China as the immobile, conservative, inward-looking, land-based civilization compared to the seafaring and adventurous West.[45] What is new in *Lang Tuteng* is that the Other is found *inside* China, among the nomads who are now surprisingly incorporated into Chinese history. Despite its descendants having conquered China from abroad, it is now explained that even Genghis Khan was Chinese. But the logic is the same. If we are to find the ego of the Chinese nation in cultural texts like these, it is in the place of the Other. *Lang Tuteng* is then not about Mongols but about the wolf-like qualities and ruthlessness of Japan and Western nations to which China has been subjected in more recent history.

Echoing the question of the hysteric in such a reading, *Lang Tuteng* essentially asks, "What is it to be a lamb?" Just like Dora's ego was found in the place of Herr K., Chinese nationalism is to be found in the Western Other. And it is not just as an ideal, but as the recognition it seeks while at the same time resisting the West's attempts to incorporate China into *its* geopolitical fantasy of kinship relations. The gaze of the narrative is that of the Other, of the Mongols, and by extension, the imperialist West, whose warlike qualities happen to be found also among the Mongols, whose approval the boys seek, and whose qualities contemporary Chinese are said to lack.

As a remedy for the virulent new Chinese nationalism, Peter Hays Gries suggested that the United States should give China more face. But is that not to treat the symptom instead of the disease? For a successful cure, the patient himself must be involved in the treatment. In this case China would need to construct a new version of its history, one that is more true to the realities of the new millennium when Chinese importance and power are rapidly increasing. Its self-bestowed role of victim not only leads to its complaining about the Others—of British, American, and Japanese imperialism, say—but implicitly is also self-denigrating. It turns into self-abasement of the type so obvious in *Lang Tuteng*.

NOTES

1. This Hegelian idea on recognition has received increasing attention in sociology with the writing of Axel Honeth but also in international relations theory (see Greenhill 2008).
2. Jiang 2004. It was translated by Howard Goldblatt in 2008 with the title, *Wolf Totem: A Novel*.
3. An abridged version of *Lang Tuteng* for secondary school students was also published under the title, *Xiao Lang, Xiao Lang* (*Little Wolf, Little Wolf*).
4. Hays Gries 2004.
5. See Slavoj Žižek 1997, 9.
6. See Michael Hunt (1983) for the early history of this special relationship.
7. Klein 2003, 2.
8. Marchetti 1993, 114. Marchetti here refers to Barbara Sichterman's book, *Femininity: The Politics of the Personal* (1986).
9. Ibid., 116.
10. See Newman 1992 for more on this American trauma.
11. Chion 2005, 95.

12. This is a path that Slavoj Žižek follows in one of his essays in *Metastasis of Enjoyment* (1996). He argues that this tendency of women to fall back into lethargy is a common Western theme and takes the notion of female depression back to the absolute negativity of Hegel's "the night of the world" (Žižek 1996, 179). Žižek's somewhat mysterious conclusion is that women represent a more primeval subject than do men.

13. His spellbinding film about the Vietnam War, *The Deer Hunter*, has already brought Cimino under criticism for right-wing loyalties and for portraying the Vietnamese as brutal and cruel.

14. Said 1985.

15. Other versions have Napoleon calling China a "giant," not a lion, and in still another quote referring to China as "she."

16. An image co-opted so eagerly by the Chinese nationalists that the symbol for Chinese liberation and rejuvenation famously became Mao Zedong looking out at the masses of Tiananmen Square declaring, "China has stood up." Although Mao did not actually utter these words at the inauguration of the People's Republic of China, people still believed they heard him vocalize the metaphor of the awakened lion (if not the alternative *sexual* metaphor referring to power, potency, and manliness).

17. During the Vietnam War younger scholars critical of John King Fairbank started to propagate Chinese agency instead. See, for example, *Discovering History in China* (2010), by Fairbank's student Paul Cohen. With China's rise, this Sinocentric, anti-Fairbankian paradigm has become dominant.

18. The novel depicts a young Chinese student's year in Japan. Sitting at the feet of the same people the Chinese derogatively called "small dwarfs" engenders feelings of inferiority. Paranoid and high-strung, the young Chinese protagonist wrongly believes that the Japanese despise him. He harbors strong, pent-up sexual feelings and dreams of the love of a woman but is obsessed with the thought that the Japanese women will recognize him as a "Chinaman" (*shinajin*). Feeling the castrating gaze of the Other, he never dares to get close to any woman; even when he visits a brothel, he does not manage to do what he has come for. Instead he gets drunk and spends the night alone. The young student contemplates revenge, connecting his sexual frustration with the state of the Chinese nation, crying out: "O China, my China, you are the cause of my death! . . . I wish you could become rich and strong soon! . . . Many, many of your children are still suffering" (Yu Dafu 1921, 45). The young man in the story decides to forget about women and devote his love to the motherland: "From now on I shall care nothing about women, absolutely nothing. I will love nothing but my country, and let my country be my love" ("Wo zai ye bu ai nürenle. Wo jiu ai wode zuguo. Wo jiu ba wode zuguo dangzuo qingren") (Ibid., 45).

19. Hsia 1971, Appendix 1, 509–33.

20. Zhong Xueping 2000.

21. Julia Lovell describes this complex in *The Politics of Cultural Capital: China's Quest for a Nobel Prize in Literature* (2006).

22. Zhang Xudong 2008.

23. However, when his compatriot Gao Xingjian was awarded the prize in 2000, Zhang Xudong voiced the opinion of Chinese intellectuals when he argued that the

West with this choice still did not recognize China. The Nobel Committee had chosen a Westernized writer who fit its projected image of China. According to Zhang, the prize signified that the West did not want to recognize the radical difference and otherness of China. See Lovell (2002) for more.

24. Mao did not hesitate to engage in risky experiments on a mass scale, starving 40 million Chinese in order to catch up with the United Kingdom in just 15 years.

25. Li Xiguang and Liu Kang 1996.

26. As argued by Ben Xu and Zhao Yiheng (1995) in two separate articles of *Ershiyi shiji* and of Wang Hui 1998.

27. Hays Gries 2004, 48.

28. For a further discussion of this, see Eng 2001, 174, 175.

29. Lacan 1993, 175.

30. Ibid., 174.

31. Ibid., 175.

32. Ibid., 176.

33. Ibid., 178.

34. As elaborated by Hegel in the preface of his *Philosophy of Right* as well as in one of the end chapters of *Phenomenology of the Spirit*. There is, of course, no pure, objective history, such as that the historian Leopold von Ranke hoped could be represented "*wie es eigentlich gewesen*" ("how it really was").

35. See Žižek 1991, 203.

36. This well-known case was first publicized by Freud in the article "From the History of an Infantile Neurosis" (1918), and later discussed and reinterpreted not only by Freud himself but, it seems, by everyone with the slightest interest in psychoanalytical theory. One of the most interesting readings of the Wolf Man case is that of Nicolas Abraham and Maria Torok (2005).

37. Central in this interpretation is another memory, that is, that the boy was seduced by his sister.

38. Freud's interpretations of dreams not only work through metaphor, metonym, and synonym; the unconscious also uses antonyms to rework the dream content (paradoxical only until we see it from a linguist's perspective).

39. An alternative interpretation perhaps would focus on this third sexual situation, one that seems to really have taken place. The young boy finds his maid on all fours, washing the floor with her derriere raised. Confronted with this scene, the boy starts to urinate. A sexual act, Freud concludes, but it is, of course, also an aggressive act. Since the maid is cleaning the floor and her young master pees on it, she is irritated and mutters something that, according to Freud, the young boy interprets as a threat of castration. Freud tries his best to link this scene to the image of the father taking the mother "doggy-style," portraying the boy's castration angst and recurrent dreams of the wolf in upright position that haunt the boy as a representation of fear of the patriarch. Freud obviously had problems with the idea that a lowly cleaning woman could instill fear in a boy.

40. The boys were sent to the countryside after the young Red Guards whom Mao Zedong had employed to wreak havoc became too belligerent. As Red Guard students they had been told by Mao to be "more martial"; for some the Cultural Revolution

meant taking part in brutal beatings of enemies of Mao as well as armed shootouts with other Red Guard units. In this sense the boys sent to the countryside were certainly well-prepared to look for martial values and symbols wherever they could find them.

41. One of the Chinese student's best friends, a stuttering young Mongol man, after a night of drinking of vodka, warns them about Mongol women. "Whe . . . whe . . . when are you going to marry a Mongol wo . . . wo . . . woman, and get a baby, born from a Mongol womb, and really count as (*suan*) a Mongol? You . . . you are too weak, not . . . not . . . not up to it (*bu xing*). Mongol women are . . . are . . . are really wild (*lihai*) when you get under the skin rug with them. More fe . . . fe . . . ferocious than the wolf. Mongol men are a . . . a . . . afraid of them, afraid as little lambs" (Jiang 2004, 34).

42. See Gao Ping, Tang Yun, Yang Yu 1997, and Hayes 2004, 77, 144, for more examples.

43. As quoted in Hays Gries 2004, 85.

44. Jiang Rong 2004, 366.

45. See Chen Xiaomei's article on Occidentalism discussing this particular TV drama of the 1980s.

Conclusion

The Gaze of the Other

Modern Chinese nationalism was always preoccupied with sexuality. From the lotus foot to the bob hairstyle, the nation was conflated with the Chinese woman—she who eventually had to give up her femininity and become a soldier saving the nation.

But the repressed reappeared with capitalism, and some of the most conspicuous changes of post-Mao China were tied to feminine fashion, new hairstyles, beauty adornment, high heels, and makeup. Gender was inscribed into the logic of consumer culture—a libidinal economy that depended on the beauty of women as communicated by glossy magazines, billboards, and TV screens.

But already by the early 1990s the All-China Women's Federation and its propaganda flagship publication, *Chinese women*, made an effort to repatriate this cultural difference. By reinventing a particular Chinese femininity, they would domesticate women twice over—first by serving husband and child and then, for the stability of the nation, by sacrificing career and ambitions in a tight job market. For this particularly *Chinese* beauty, qualities like softness and shyness were stressed. Consumer culture and state-controlled media spoke with one and the same voice as advertisements for Chinese and foreign beauty products delivered images of an understated attractiveness while the multinational *Elle* became *the* glossy fashion magazine contributing to bringing about the promised internationalization of a still fledgling fashion industry.

As the Maoist regime collapsed, the Chinese had to engage seriously in its imaginary relations with the outside world. Uncertainties about China's real international status forced émigré Chinese to arbitrate between the big Other of a neoliberal Western-centric order and the national subject. It was, therefore, often Chinese-Americans who were put in the position of explaining Chinese's shortcomings in this new libidinal economy. In the authoritative *Chinese women*, one such Chinese-American, Zhao Haosheng, doubted that there existed any real women in China. Another, Kan Yue-sai, took it upon herself to make Venus appear on the Chinese shore. The importance of the foreign Other's admiration of Chinese women was furthermore highlighted in beauty product and fashion advertising and editorials alike.

The government shared this aspiration as the success of a Chinese clothing industry on the international scene became a state-sponsored project. In fashion magazines, images of modest models and clothes were mixed with hyperbolic language about how Western designers had been waiting for the moment when Chinese women would make these beautiful dresses of international fashion look even better.

There was also, however, tangible anxiety in the perceived lack of a Chinese femininity. After long isolation from the outside world and under a stern communist sexual regime of "weakening men and strengthening women," female beauty became an issue connected with recognition from the foreign Other.

With Deng Xiaoping's Reform and Open Door policy, a flow of Chinese students was going abroad. Being in such close proximity to the Western Other proved traumatic. After decades of being fed Maoist propaganda on how the capitalist world was close to collapse and ripe for a Chinese-inspired world revolution, these émigrés faced the Real of geopolitical might. Their sense of discomfort was not, however, so much with the realization that the West was rich, powerful, and well-off; it was with the discovery that China was not looked up to as they had been led to believe, that the Other's gaze was disapproving and patronizing.

This gaze of the Western Other saw in the Chinese something eliding its own introspection, something "more in me than myself." This disturbing lack of identity became an important psychological factor in popular Chinese nationalism, and the experiences of Chinese living abroad needed only a push for a retreat back into the Republican-era "obsession with China." As émigré literature appeared in the early 1990s and became the PRC's first commercially mass-marketed book genre, it was quickly recast into television soap operas that reached a huge audience. These showed not only the real mistreatment that Chinese suffered in the West but also fueled vengeful fantasies of exaggerated success stories in which blonde, blue-eyed women were made to satisfy Chinese men. Getting intimate with the racial fetish of the white woman was not without its danger, however, as it often came too close to revealing the emptiness behind this fantasy-support of the Chinese subject.

Reform era advertising presented two contradictory sets of female images. Asian women were portrayed as subordinate, extremely feminine, and childish, while Western women were strong, masculine, and uninhibited. The different representations reflected a certain libidinal logic of international relations, revealing a racial fetishism that centers on possession or lack of the same skin color. The white woman in China's imaginations discloses an economy of nationalist desire in which anxiety over the Other's gaze results in destabilization of the national identity. The use of the fetish of the white woman in this context furthermore functions as a denial of reality, as well as a triumph over and psychological safeguard against the threat of castration posed by a still mighty "West."

Certainly under the influence of a Western imaginary, two recurring themes repeatedly pop up in Chinese popular texts from the 1990s. One is about having or not having the symbolic phallus. The second is about the gaze of the Other. The two relate to each other in how Chinese people viewed the West and the resulting new, popular nationalism. They detected in the gaze of the Other a peril of the West demonizing China, of "them" wanting to stop "our" rise to riches and glory. The imagined kingdom of Mao was in ruins, and China was reinstated into the symbolic of international relations. The reply of CCP propaganda to the new situation was to once again portray China as threatened, to recast it as the rape victim from a "century of humiliation."

The expressions of this new nationalism came to resemble the discourse of Freud's female hysteric, pondering the question of her identity under the power of a male gaze, trying to figure out what the male observer sees when he looks at her—in both cases a resistance to the symbolic order. The validity of this interpretation of China as female hysteric is affirmed by "the obsession with China," the "Nobel complex," and other messages of a Chinese nationalistic desire for recognition. All these attempts to find one's own ego in the gaze of the Other are analog with how China's new nationalism conceived of Chinese identity, that is, how a Western Other perceived the country. But behind this mirroring in the Ideal-Ego of the Other and the narcissistic aggression directed toward that space lies anxiety. The fact is that from behind the screen of fantasies, at the very moment one comprehends that the Other is actually returning the gaze, the Real appears. This castrating gaze unravels any narcissistic projections of a full identity exactly when it has to confront not just the symbolic of international relations, but the traumatic Real. As illustrated by a number of popular Chinese narratives on sexual encounters with Westerners, the gaze of the Other that has been desired so fervently turns into a frightening encounter instead with Medusa's head.

This double investment—for recognition and for love—in the gaze of the Other is bound to repeatedly produce the same outburst of demand for appreciation, followed in a never-ending dialectic of hysteric eruptions of nationalism and identity anxiety. In order for the new Chinese nationalism to become a strength, China would be better off turning its focus away from the Ideal-Ego of the Other to rework and reinterpret its own history as a new, *truly* non-Western-centric discourse. The victim narrative has outlived its usefulness; China now needs to look back and reflect in order to be able to look forward with confidence.

References

FILMS, THEATER PLAYS, AND TELEVISION SHOWS

Cimino, Michael. *Year of the Dragon*, movie. 1985. Hollywood: MGM/United Artists.

Cronenberg, David. *M. Butterfly*, movie. 1993. Hollywood: Warner Brothers.

Feng Xiaogan, Zheng Xiaolang. *Beijingren zai niuyue* (*A Beijing Man in New York*), TV series. 1993. Beijing: China Central Television and Beijing Television.

Hwang, David Henry. *M. Butterfly*, theater play, premiered 1988 on the Eugene O'Neill Theatre, Broadway.

King, Henry. *Love Is a Many-Splendored Thing*, Movie. 1955. Twentieth Century-Fox.

Quine, Richard. *The World of Suzie Wong*, movie. 1960. Paramount Pictures.

Sun Sha. *Eluosi gunian zai Harbin* (*Russian Girls in Harbin*), TV series. 1994. CCTV and Heilongjiang Studio/Tian'e Film.

Wang Binlin, Li Jinxian. *Yangniu'er zai Beijing* (*Foreign Babes in Beijing*), TV series. 1996. Beijing Film Studio.

Wise, Robert. *The Sand Pebbles*, movie. 1966. Hollywood: Twentieth Century Fox Film Corporation.

PRINTED MATERIAL

Abraham, Nicolas and Maria Torok. *The Wolf Man's Magic Word: A Cryptonymy*. Minneapolis: University of Minnesota Press, 2005.

Ai Bei. *Red Ivy, Green Earth Mother: Stories by Ai Bei*. iUniverse, 2000.

Anderson, Benedict. *Imagined Communities: Reflections on the Origins and Spread of Nationalism*. New York: Verso, 1991 (1983).

Appadurai, Arjun. "Disjuncture and Difference." In *Global Cultures*, edited by Mike Featherstone, 295–310. London: Sage, 1990.

Balfour, Freddie. "Patience Now, Profits Later." *Far Eastern Economic Review*, no. 11 (September 1986): 166–67.

Ballerino Cohen, Colleen, Richard Wilk, and Beverly Stoeltje, eds. *Beauty Queens on the Global Stage: Gender, Contests, and Power*. New York: Routledge, 1996.

Barmé, Geremie R. "To Screw Foreigners Is Patriotic: China's Avant-garde Nationalists." *The China Journal*, no. 34 (1995): 209–34.

Baughman, Cynthia. "Elle looks to the East; Move over Mao Suits: Patricia Wang Is Introducing High Style." *Folio: The Magazine for Magazine Management*. Media Central Inc., 1988.

"Beauty and the East." *Beijing* 2 (1995).

Belk, Russell W. "Third World Consumer Culture." In *Research in Marketing: Marketing and Development: Toward Broader Dimensions*, edited by Erdoğan Kumcu and A. Fuat Firat, 103–27. Greenwich, CT: JAI Press, 1988.

Belk, Russell W., David K. Tse, and Nan Zhou. "Becoming a Consumer Society: A Longitudinal and Cross-Cultural Content Analysis of Print Ads from Hong Kong, the People's Republic of China and Taiwan." *Journal of Consumer Research* 15, no. 4 (March 1989): 457–72.

Bennett, David. "Libidinal Economy, Prostitution and Consumer Culture." *Textual Practice* 24, no. 1 (2010): 93–121.

Berger Peter L. and Thomas Luckmann. *The Social Construction of Reality: A Treatise in the Sociology of Knowledge*. London: Penguin Books, 1966.

Bhabha, Homi K. *The Location of Culture*. London: Routledge, 1994.

Bordo, Susan. *Unbearable Weight: Feminism, Western Culture, and the Body*. Berkeley: University of California Press, 1993.

Brownell, Susan. "The Body and the Beautiful in Chinese Nationalism: Sportswomen and Fashion Models in the Reform Era." *China Information* 12, nos. 2–3 (Autumn–Winter 1998): 36–59.

Brownell, Susan. 1996. "Representing Gender in the Chinese nation: Chinese Sportswomen and Beijing's Bid for the 2000 Olympics." *Identities* 283.

Brumberg, Joan Jacobs. *The Body Project: An Intimate History of American Girls*. New York: Random House, 1997.

Buruma, Ian and Avishai Margalit. *Occidentalism: The West in the Eyes of Its Enemies*. Penguin Books 2005.

Butler, Judith. *Gender Trouble: Feminism and the Subversion of Identity*. New York: Routledge, 1990.

Campbell, Colin. *The Romantic Ethic and the Spirit of Modern Consumerism*. Oxford, UK: B. Blackwell, 1987.

Cao Guilin. *Beijingren zai niuyue* (*A Beijinger in New York*). Beijing: Xinhua shudian zongdian, 1992.

Chadwick, James. "Navigating through China's new advertising law: the role of marketing research." *International Journal of Advertising* 16, no. 4 (1997): 284–94.

Chai, Joseph C. H. "Consumption and Living Standards in China." *China Quarterly* 131 (September 1992): 721–49.

Chen Xiaomei. *Occidentalism: A Theory of Counter-Discourse in Post-Mao China*. Oxford University Press, 1995.

Chen Yun. "Chi qingchun fan de nühai" ("Girls Eating from the Ricebowl of Youth"). *Zhongguo funü* (October 1993): 37.

Cheng, Allen Tien-jen. "Prying Into China." *Asia Inc.* (October 1995).

Cheng Ying. "Zhonghua da xuanmei" ("Great Chinese Beauty Contests"). *Jiushi Niandai* (May 1993).

China: Consumer Trends. Beijing: New Star Publishers, 1993.

Chion, Michel. Translated by Robert Julian. *David Lynch*. London: BFI Pub., 2005.

Chow, Rey. Edited with intro, eds. "*On Chineseness as a Theoretical Problem*." *boundary 2* (Special Issue on Modern Chinese Literary and Cultural Studies in the Age of Theory) 25, no. 3 (Fall 1998): 1–24.

Chow, Rey. *Woman and Chinese Modernity: The Politics of Reading between West and East*. Minneapolis: University of Minnesota Press, 1991.

Clark, Hazel. "The Cheung Sam: Issues of Fashion and Cultural Identity." In *China Chic: East Meets West*, edited by Valerie Steele and John S. Major, 155–65. New Haven, CT: Yale University Press, 1999.

"Cong guanggao ni kandaole shenmeyangde nüren" ("What Kind of Women Do You Find in Advertising"). *Sanlian shenghuo zhoukan* 4, no. ? (1997): 24–25.

Craik, Jennifer. *The Face of Fashion: Cultural Studies in Fashion*. London: Routledge, 1994.

Creighton, Millie. "Imagining the Other in Japanese Advertising Campaigns." In *Occidentalism: Images of the West*, edited by James Carrier. New York: Oxford University Press, 1995.

Croll, Elisabeth. *China's New Consumers: Social Development and Domestic Demand*. London: Routledge, 2006.

Croll, Elisabeth. *Changing Identities of Chinese Women: Rhetoric, Experience and Self-Perception in 20th Century China*. London: Zed Books, 1995.

Crowell, Todd and David Hsieh. "Little Emperors: Is China's One Child Policy Creating a Society of Brats?" *Asiaweek* 21, no. 48 (December 1, 1995): 44–50.

Cunningham, Susan. "Traditional Attitudes Permeate Hong Kong Materialism." *Asian Advertising and Marketing* (February 1990): 24–27.

Dai Jinhua. *Cinema and Desire: Feminist Marxism and Cultural Politics in the Work of Dai Jinhua*, edited by Jing Wang and Tani E. Barlow. London: Verso, 2002.

Dai Jinhua. "Invisible Writing: The Politics of Chinese Mass Culture in the 1990s." *Modern Chinese Literature and Culture* 11, no. 1 (Spring 1999): 31–60.

Davies, Deborah S. *The Consumer Revolution in Urban China*. Berkeley: University of California Press, 2000.

Davis, Deborah S. and Julia S. Sensenbrenner. "Commercializing Childhood: Parental Purchases for Shanghai's Only Child". In *The Consumer Revolution in Urban China*, ed. Deborah S. Davis, 54–79. Berkeley: University of California Press, 2000.

Dikötter, Frank. *Sex, Culture and Modernity in China: Medical Science and the Construction of Sexual Identities in the Early Republican Period*. Hong Kong: Hong Kong University Press, 1995.

Dikötter, Frank. *The Discourse of Race in Modern China*. Hong Kong: Hong Kong University Press, 1992.

Ding Yunpeng. "Wei guanggao zheng ming" ("Restoring the Good Name of Advertising"). *Wenhuibao* 14, (January 1979).

Douglas, Mary. *Natural Symbols: Explorations in Cosmology*. Routledge (1970) 2013.

Duara, Prasenjit. "The Regime of Authenticity: Timelessness, Gender and National History in Modern China." *History and Theory* 37, no. 3 (October 1998): 287–308.

Duara, Prasenjit. "De-Constructing the Chinese Nation." In *Chinese Nationalism*, edited by Jonathan Unger, 31–55. Armonk, NY: M. E. Sharpe. 1996.

Duara, Prasenjit. *Rescuing History from the Nation: Questioning Narratives of Modern China*. Chicago: University of Chicago Press, 1995.

Eberhard, Wolfram. *A Dictionary of Chinese Symbols: Hidden Symbols in Chinese Life and Thought*. London: Routledge & Kegan Paul, 1986.

Eberhard, Wolfram. "What is Beautiful in a Chinese Woman?" In *Moral and Social Values of the Chinese; Collected Essays*. Taipei, Taiwan: Ch'eng-wen Pub. Co., 1971.

Ebrey, Patricia. "Women, Marriage, and the Family in Chinese History." In *Heritage of China*. Edited by Paul Ropp, 197–223. Berkeley: University of California Press, 1990.

"*ELLE* Grows Despite Tighter Local Market." *Media Asia* (July 9, 1993).

Emerson, Tony. "Global Ball." *Newsweek*, April 1996, 47.

Eng, David L. *Racial Castration: Managing Masculinity in Asian America*. Durham, NC: Duke University Press, 2001.

Evans, Harriet. *Women and Sexuality in China: Female Sexuality and Gender since 1949*. New York: Continuum, 1997.

Ewen, Stuart. *Captains of Consciousness: Advertising and the Social Roots of the Consumer Culture*. New York: McGraw-Hill, 1976.

Ewen, Stuart and Elisabeth Ewen. *Channels of Desire: Mass Images and the Shaping of American Consciousness*. New York: McGraw-Hill, 1982.

"False Advertising Angers Consumers." *Beijing Review* no. 30 (July 1985): 8–9.

Fan Lianfeng. "Jin Yuxi: Xiangei dongfang nüxingde ai" ("Kan Yue-sai: A Dedication of Love for Oriental Women"). *Zhongguo funü* (June 1993): 39.

Fang Yi. 1995. "Yizhi hong chungao" ("A Red Lipstick"). *Shaonü* 57 (1995): 24–25.

Fanon, Frantz. *Black Skin, White Masks*. New York: Grove Press, 1967.

Farrer, James. *Opening Up: Youth, Sex, Culture, and Market Reform in Shanghai*. University of Chicago Press, 2002

"Fractured Images: Have Chinese Women Lost Their Way in the Pursuit of Western Ideals of Beauty?" *Window* (April 14, 1995): 32–37.

Featherstone, Mike. *Consumer Culture and Postmodernism*. London: Sage, 1991.

Featherstone, Mike. "Consumer Culture, Symbolic Power, and Universalism." *Mass Culture, Popular Culture, and Social Life in the Middle East*. Boulder, CO: Westview Press, 1987.

Featherstone, Mike. "The Body in Consumer Culture." *Theory, Culture & Society* 1, no. 1 (Spring 1982): 18–33.

Finnane, Antonia. *Changing Clothes in China: Fashion, History, Nation*. New York: Columbia University Press, 2008.

Finnane, Antonia. "China on the Catwalk: Between Economic Success and Nationalist Anxiety."*The China Quarterly*, 183 (September 2005): 587–608.

Finnane, Antonia. "Military Culture and Chinese dress in the Early Twentieth Century." In *China Chic: East Meets West*, edited by Valerie Steele and John S. Major. New Haven: Yale University Press, 1999.

Finnane, Antonia. "What Should Chinese Women Wear? A National Problem." *Modern China* 22, no. 2 (April 1996): 115–66.

Fitzgerald, John. "The Nationless State: The Search for a Nation in Modern Chinese Nationalism." In *Chinese Nationalism*, edited by Jonathan Unger, 56–85. Armonk, NY: M. E. Sharpe, Inc., 1996.

Forney, Matt. 1996. "Hoop Nightmares." *Far Eastern Economic Review* 159, no. 51 (December 19, 1996): 64.

Forney, Matt. "Left Behind in the Countryside." *Newsweek* Asia edition (August 21, 1995): 12–13.

Freud, Sigmund. *Aus der Geschichte einer infantilen Neurose* (*From the History of an Infantile Neurosis*). Leipzig: Internationaler Psychoanalytischer Verlag, 1924. Reprinted in *The Freud Reader*, edited by Peter Gay. London: Vintage, 1995.

Freud, Sigmund. "Fetishism." *The Standard Edition of the Complete Psychological Works of Sigmund Freud*, 7, (1927): 147–58.

Freud, Sigmund. (1916–1917g [1915]) "Trauer und Melancholie," *Intern. Zschr. ärztl. Psychoanal 4*, 277–87; *G.W.*, 10, 428–48; Mourning and melancholia. *SE*, 14: 243–58.

Friedman, Jonathan. "Being in the World: Globalization and Localization." *Theory, Culture and Society* 7 (1990): 311–28.

Gao Ping, Tang Yun, and Yang Yu. *Xuezhai: Dui Riben suopei jishi* (*Blood Debt: Chinese Claims for Repatriations*). Beijing: Guoji wenhua chuban gongsi, 1997.

Gao Yunxiang. "Nationalist and Feminist Discourses on Jianmei (Robust Beauty) during China's 'National Crisis' in the 1930s." *Gender & History* 18, issue 3, (2006): 546–73.

Garnaut, Ross and Guonan Ma. "How Rich Is China? Evidence from the Food Economy." *The Australian Journal of Chinese Affairs* no. 30 (July 1993): 121–46.

Gee, Alison Dakota. "The Price of Beauty." *Asiaweek* (August 2, 1996): 38.

Gellner, Ernest. *Nations and Nationalism*. Ithaca, NY: Cornell University Press, 1983.

Gerth, Karl. *China Made: Consumer Culture and the Creation of the Nation*. Cambridge, MA: Harvard University Asia Center, 2003.

Giddens, Anthony. *Modernity and Self-Identity: Self and Society in the Late Modern Age*. Cambridge, UK: Polity Press, 1991.

Goffman, Erving. *Gender Advertisements*. New York: Harper & Row, 1979.

Goldman, Robert. *Reading Ads Socially*. London: Routledge, 1992.

Goodman, David S. G. "The People's Republic of China: The Party-State, Capitalist Revolution and New Entrepreneurs." In *The New Rich In Asia: Mobile Phones, McDonalds and Middle-class Revolution*, edited by Richard Robison and David S. G. Goodman. London: New York: Routledge, 1996.

Green, Adam Isaiah. "The Social Organization of Desire: The Sexual Fields Approach." Sociological Theory. 26 (2008): 25–50.

"Guanggaode shengming zaiyu zhenshi" ("The Survival of Advertising Rests on Its Truthfulness"). *Renmin Ribao* (January 31, 1981).

"Guowuyuan banbu: Guanggao guanli tiaoli" ("Promulgation from the State Council: Rules and Regulations for Managing Advertising"). In *Guojia gongshang xingzheng guanliju guanggaosi, Zhongguo guanggao fagui huibian* (*A Compilation of Rules and Regulations for Advertising in China*). Beijing: Zhongguo kexue jishu chubanshe (China Science and Technology Publishing House), 1993.

Greenfeld, Liah. 1990. "The Formation of the Russian National Identity: The Role of Status Insecurity and *Ressentiment*." *Comparative Studies in Society and History* 32, no. 3 (July 1990): 549–91.

"Hachette Appoints Publisher." *South China Morning Post* (June 17, 1998).

"Hachette Steps up Frequency of Publication for *Elle* China in Response to Market Demand." *Asian Advertising and Marketing* (Oct. 1, 1993).

Hakim, Catherine. "Erotic Capital." *European Sociological Review*, 26 (2010): 499–518.

"Haiwai jiechu nü huaren yingping tianshi Jin Yuxi" ("An Outstanding Chinese Abroad, the Angel on Television: Kan Yue-sai"). *Shijie shizhuang zhiyuan* (*A Garden of World Fashion*) (Spring 1989).

Harrison, Henrietta. 2001. *China. Series: Inventing the Nation*. London: Arnold; New York: Co-published in the United States of America by Oxford University Press, 2001.

Harvey, David. *A Brief History of Neoliberalism*. Oxford University Press, 2007.

Hays Gries, Peter. *China's New Nationalism: Pride, Politics, and Diplomacy*. Berkeley: University of California Press, 2004.

Hegel, Georg Wilhelm Friedrich. *Outlines of the Philosophy of Right*. Translated by T. M. Knox; revised, edited, and introduced by Stephen Houlgate. Oxford: Oxford University Press, 2008.

Hegel, Georg Wilhelm Friedrich. *Phenomenology of the Spirit*. Translated by A. V. Miller; with analysis of the text and foreword by J. N. Findlay. Oxford: Clarendon Press, 1977.

Ho, Virgil Kit-yiu. "The Limits of Hatred: Popular Cantonese Attitudes Towards the West in the 1920s and the Early 1930s." *East Asian History*, no. 2 (1991): 87–104.

Hong Fan and J. A. Mangan. "From Chinese Cripples to Chinese Champions: Footbinding, Freedom and Femininity." *IIAS Newsletter* 11 (Winter 1997): 34.

Hong Junhao. "The Resurrection of Advertising in China: Developments, Problems, and Trends." *Asian Survey* 34, no. 4 (April 1994): 326–42.

Honig, Emily and Gail Hershatter. *Personal Voices: Chinese Women in the 1980s*. Stanford, CA: Stanford University Press, 1988.

Hooper, Beverley. "Women, Consumerism and the State in Post Mao China." *Asian Studies Review* 17, no. 3 (1994): 73–83.

Hsia, Chih-tsing. *A History of Modern Chinese Fiction*. New Haven, CT: Yale University Press, 1971.

Huang Ping. "New Dilemmas About Consumerism." *China Daily*, October 12, 1995.

Huang Ping. "Xiaofei zhuyi zai dangdai zhongguo" ("Consumerism in Contemporary China"). *1994 "zhongri "shichang jingji yu wenhua" xueshu yanjiuhui lunwenji* (*A Collection of Articles from the Chinese-Japanese Scholarly Conference on Market Economy and Culture 1994*) 1995.

Huang Yu. "Peaceful Evolution: The Case of Television Reform in Post-Mao China." *Media, Culture & Society* 16 (1994): 217–41.

Human Rights in China. *Caught Between Tradition and the State: Violations of the Human Rights of Chinese Women.* New York: Human Rights in China, 1995.

Hunt Michael H. *The Making of a Special Relationship: The United States and China to 1914.* Columbia University Press, 1983.

Ikenberry, John. "The Rise of China, the United States, and the Future of Liberal International Order." In *Tangled Titans: The United States and China*, edited by David Shambaugh. Lanham, MD: Rowman & Littlefield, 2013.

"It's Offical—Ads Pull the Punches in China." *Asian Advertising and Marketing* (June 3, 1994): 6.

Jameson, Fredric. 1993. "Starka tolkningar segrar" (The Victory of Strong Interpretations). *Res Publica* 24 (December 1993): 19–44.

Jiang Rong. *Lang tuteng* (*Wolf totem*). Wuhan: Changjiang wenyi chubanshe, 2004.

"Kandeng guanggao ye ying yange shencha" ("Print Advertising Need Also to Be Seriously Inspected"). *Renmin Ribao* (May 18, 1985).

Kam Louie. *Theorising Chinese Masculinity: Society and Gender in China.* Cambridge: Cambridge University Press, 2002.

Karp, Jonathan. "Cast of Thousands." *Far Eastern Economic Review* (January 27, 1994).

Karp, Jonathan. "Prime Time Police." *Far Eastern Economic Review* (October 21, 1993).

"Kick Off, Cash In." *Far Eastern Economic Review* (Jan. 16 , 1997): 46–50.

Klein, Christina. *Cold War Orientalism: Asia in the Middlebrow Imagination, 1945–1961.* University of California, 2003.

Ko, Dorothy. *Cinderella's Sisters: A Revisionist History of Footbinding*, Berkeley, University of California, 2005.

Ko, Dorothy. 1997. "The Body as Attire: The Shifting Meanings of Footbinding in Seventeenth Century China." *Journal of Women's History* 8, no. 4 (Winter 1997): 8–27.

Kondo, Dorinne. 1992. "The Aesthetics and Politics of Japanese Identity in the Fashion Industry." In *Remade in Japan: Everyday Life and Consumer Taste in a Changing Society*, edited by Joseph J. Tobin. New Haven, CT: Yale University Press, 1992.

Kong Liang and Lawrence W. Jacobs. "China's Advertising: Education and Research is the Key." *International Journal of Advertising* 12, no. 2 (1993).

Kunz, Jean Lock. "From Maoism to *Elle*: The Impact of Political Ideology on Fashion Trends in China." *International Sociology* 11, no. 3 (September 1996): 317–35.

Lacan, Jacques. *The Seminar of Jacques Lacan: The Psychoses (Book III).* Translated by Jacques-Alain Miller and Russell Grigg. London: Routledge, 1993.

Lacan, Jacques. *The Seminar of Jacques Lacan: The Ethics of Psychoanalysis (Book VII).* Translated by D. Porter. London: Routledge, 1992.

Lacan, Jacques. *The Seminar of Jacques Lacan: The Ego in Freud's Theory and in the Technique of Psychoanalysis (Book II).* New York: Norton, 1991.

Lacan, Jacques. *Ecrits: A Selection.* Translated by Alan Sheridan. New York: Norton, 1977a.

Lacan, Jacques. *The Seminar. Book XI. The Four Fundamental Concepts of Psychoanalysis.* Translated by Alan Sheridan. London: Hogarth Press, 1977b.

Laermans, Rudi. "Learning to Consume: Early Department Stores and the Shaping of the Modern Consumer Culture (1860–1914)." *Theory, Culture and Society* 10 (1993): 79–102.

Lasch, Christopher. *The Culture of Narcissism: American Life in an Age of Diminishing Expectations.* New York: Warner Books, 1979.

Li Xiaoping. "Fashioning the Body in Post-Mao China." In *Consuming Fashion: Adoring the Transnational Body*, edited by Anne Brydon and Sandra Niessen, 71–90. Oxford: Berg, 1998.

Li Xiao. "Wode xuanze you shenme budui" ("What's Wrong with My Decision?"). "Under the heading "Guanyu 'qingchun fan' de huati" ("About 'Eating the Fruits of Youth'"). *Zhongguo funü* (January 1994): 10.

Li Xiguang and Liu Kang. *Yaomuhua Zhongguo de beiho* (*The Plot to Demonize China*). Beijing: Zhongguo shehui kexue chubanshe, 1996.

Li Yaoming. 1993. "Dalu huangchao gungun lai" ("The Yellow Waves Keep Rolling in on the Mainland"). *Jiushi niandai* (June 1993): 44–49.

Lin, Carolyn A. "Cultural Differences in Message Strategies: A Comparison between American and Japanese TV Commercials." *Journal of Advertising Research* 33, no. 4 (July–August 1993): 40–48.

Lin Lin. "Huazhuang de wuqu" ("Mistakes in Putting on Make-up"). *Xiaofeizhe,* ("Consumers") 1 (1994): 13.

Lin Yutang. *My Country and My People.* New York: Reynal & Hitchcock, 1935.

Liu Kang. "Popular Culture and the Culture of the Masses in Contemporary China." *Boundary 2* 24 no. 3 (1997): 99–122.

Liu Ning. "Nüren, bu yao bei qingchun zhuyi suo kunhuo" ("Women, do not let youthism confuse you"). Zhongguo funü (April 1994): 36.

Liu Shengzhi. *Dang dai nüxing zazhi de wen hua yan jiu* (*Cultural Studies on Contemporary Women's Magazines*). Guangxi shi fan da xue chu ban she: Guilin, 2007.

Liu Xiaoou. "Zhongguo wu nüren" ("China Has No Women"). *Hunyin yu jiating* (March 1995): 40–41.

Lovell, Julia. *The Opium War: Drugs, Dreams and the Making of China.* New York: Picador, 2011.

Lovell. Julia. http://thechinabeat.blogspot.com.br/2009/04/its-just-history-patriotic-education-in.html.

Lovell, Julia. *The Politics of Cultural Capital: China's Quest for a Nobel Prize in Literature.* Honolulu: University of Hawaii Press, 2006.

Lovell, Julia. "Gao Xingjian, the Nobel Prize and Chinese Intellectuals: Notes on the Aftermath of the Nobel Prize 2000." *Modern Chinese Literature and Culture* 14, no. 2 (Fall 2002): 1–50.

Lu, Sheldon. *Chinese Modernity and Global Biopolitics: Studies in Literature and Visual Culture.* Honolulu: University of Hawai'i Press, 2007.

Lull, James. *China Turned On: Television, Reform, and Resistance.* London; New York: Routledge, 1991.

Lury, Celia. *Consumer Culture*. New Brunswick, NJ: Rutgers University Press, 1996.
Lynne, Curry. "How to Tap China's Elite." *Advertising Age* (December 14, 1981).
Lyric, Hughes. "Door is Open to U.S." *Advertising Age* (June 1986): 57.
MacMillan, Margaret. *Nixon and Mao: The Week that Changed the World*. New York: Random House, 2007.
"Madison Avenue in China." *San Francisco Chronicle* (March 25, 1979).
"Mainland Women Willing to Absorb Fashion Trends." *South China Morning Post* (February 15, 1995).
Mann, Susan. *Gender and Sexuality in Modern Chinese History*. New York: Cambridge University Press, 2011.
Mao, A. "Hei pifu bu bi dade tai bai" ("Don't Make Dark Skin Too White"). *Funü zhi you* (March 1994): 46.
Mao Zedong. *Mao's Road to Power: Revolutionary Writings 1912–1949, vol. 1: The Pre-Marxist Period, 1912–1920*. Edited by Stuart R. Schram. Armonk: M. E. Sharpe, 1992.
Marchetti, Gina. *Romance and the "Yellow Peril": Race, Sex, and Discursive Strategies in Hollywood Fiction*. Berkeley: University of California Press, 1993.
Markand, Frankel and Kari Huus. "All the Nudes that Fit to Print." *Newsweek* (August 30, 1993).
McCracken, Ellen. *Decoding Women's Magazines: From Mademoiselle to Ms.* Houndmills, Basingstoke, Hampshire: MacMillan, 1993.
McCracken, Grant David. *Culture and Consumption: New Approaches to the Symbolic Character of Consumer Goods and Activities*. Bloomington: Indiana University Press, 1988.
McDowell, Colin. *McDowell's Directory of Twentieth Century Fashion*. London: Frederick Mueller, 1984.
McKillop, Peter. "Seeking Salvation Near Home." *Newsweek* (August 30, 1993): 25.
McLaren, Anne E.. "Chinese Cultural Revivalism: Changing Gender Constructions in the Yangtze River Delta." In *Gender and Power in Affluent Asia*, edited by Krishna Sen and Maila Stivens, 195–221. London: Routledge, 1998.
Meng Yue. "Female Images and National Myth." In *Gender Politics in Modern China: Writing and Feminism*, edited by Tani E. Barlow, 118–36. Durham: Duke University Press, 1993.
Meyer, Mahlan. "Crown of Thorns." *South China Morning Post* (July 21, 2002).
Miller, Laura. *Beauty Up: Exploring Contemporary Japanese Beauty Aesthetics*. Berkeley: University of California Press, 2006.
Mo Yan. *Feng ru fei dun* (*Big Breasts, Wide Hips*). Beijing: Zuojia chubanshe, 1995.
The Modern Girl around the World Research Group, Alys Eve Weinbaum, Lynn M. Thomas, Priti Ramamurthy, Uta G. Poiger, Madeleine Yue Dong (eds.) *The Modern Girl Around the World: Consumption, Modernity, and Globalization*. Duke University Press Books, 2008.
"Move over Darling: Special Focus, Magazines in Asia." *Asian Advertising and Marketing* (January 12, 1996).
Mulvey, Laura. "Visual Pleasures and Narrative Cinema." *Screen* 16, no. 3 (1975): 6–18.
Munshi, Shoma, ed. *Images of the 'Modern Woman' in Asia: Global Media, Local Meanings*. Richmond: Curzon, 2001.

Newman, Robert P. *Owen Lattimore and the "Loss" of China.* Berkeley: University of California Press, 1992.

Ng Chun Bong, Cheuk Pak Tong, Wong Ying, and Yvonne Lo. *Duhui Modeng: Yuefenpai 1910–1930.* Hong Kong: Joint Publishing, 1994.

Ong, Aihwa and Donald Nonini, eds. *Ungrounded Empires: The Cultural Politics of Modern Chinese Transnationalism.* New York: Routledge, 1997.

"Photo Opportunity Kodak, Fuji Face Off in Neutral Territory: China's Vast Market." *Wall Street Journal Europe* (May 29, 1996).

Pollay, Richard W. "The Distorted Mirror: Reflections on the Unintended Consequences of Advertising." *Journal of Marketing* 50, no. 2 (1986): 18–36.

Pollay, Richard W. "Twentieth Century Advertising: Determinants of Informativeness. *Written Communication* 1, no. 1 (1983): 56–77.

Radner, Hilary. *Shopping Around: Feminist Culture and the Pursuit of Pleasure.* New York: Routledge, 1994.

Reaves, Lynne. "China: A New Frontier for Advertisers." *Advertising Age* (September 16, 1985).

Reaves, Lynne. "China Market Still Hot Despite Setbacks." *Advertising Age* (June 9, 1986).

Rice, Marshall D. and Lu Zaiming. "A Content Analysis of Chinese Magazine Advertisements." *Journal of Advertising* 17, no. 4 (1988): 43–48.

Rofel, Lisa. *Desiring China: Experiments in Neoliberalism, Sexuality, and Public Culture.* Durham: Duke University Press, 2007.

Rubin, Gayle. "The Traffic in Women: Notes on the Political Economy of Sex." In *Literary Theory: An Anthology* (2nd ed.). Edited by Julie Rivkin and Michael Ryan, 770–94. Malden, MA: Blackwell, 2004.

Said, Edward W. *Orientalism.* London: Penguin Books, 1985.

"Sanshisui kuai hufu!" ("Thirty years old, hurry to protect your skin!") *Nübao* (January 1996): 23.

Schein, Louisa. "Gender and Internal Orientalism in China." *Modern China* 23, no. 1 (January 1997): 69–98.

Schein, Louisa. "The Consumption of Color and the Politics of White Skin in Post-Mao China." *Social Text*, no. 41 (Winter 1994): 141–64.

Schell, Orville. *To Get Rich Is Glorious: China in the Eighties.* New York: Pantheon, 1984.

Semenik, Richard J., Nan Zhou, and William L. Moore. "Chinese Managers' Attitudes Toward Advertising in China." *Journal of Advertising* 15, no. 4. (1986): 56–62.

Seno, Alexandra A. 1998. "When Weird Does Not Work." *Asiaweek* (July 31, 1988).

"Shenme shi xiandai nüxing mei?" ("What Is the Beauty of Modern Women?") *Zhongguo funü* (August 1991).

Shilling, Chris. *The Body and Social Theory.* London: SAGE, 2012.

Sichtermann, Barbara. *Femininity: The Politics of the Personal.* Minneapolis: University of Minnesota Press, 1986.

Slater, Don. *Consumer Culture and Modernity.* Cambridge, UK: Polity Press, 1997.

Sommers, Mathew. *Sex, Law, and Society in Late Imperial China.* Stanford University Press, 2002.

Song Qiang, Zhang Zangzang, and Qiao Bian. *Zhongguo keyi shuo bu (China Can Say No)*. Beijing: Lianhe Chubanshe, 1996.
Stavrakakis, Yannis. *Lacan and the Political*. London; New York: Routledge, 1999.
Steele, Valerie and John S. Major. *China Chic: East Meets West*. New Haven: Yale University Press, 1999.
Stevenson, H. L. "Chinese Worried About Ad Growth." *Advertising Age* (September 16, 1985).
Stewart, Sally & Nigel Campbell. "Advertising in China and Hong Kong: A Preliminary Study." *International Journal of Advertising*, 7 (1988).
Stewart, Sally and Nigel Campbell. "Advertising in Mainland China: A Preliminary Study." *International Journal of Advertising* 5, no. 4 (1986).
Stoler, Ann Lara. *Carnal Knowledge and Imperial Power: Race and the Intimate in Colonial Rule*. Berkeley: University of California Press, 2002.
Stross, Randall E. *Bulls in the China Shop and Other Sino-American Business Encounters*. Honolulu: University of Hawaii Press, 1993.
Stross, Randall. "The Return of Advertising in China." *China Quarterly* 123 (September 1990): 485–502.
Sun Lung-kee. "The Politics of Hair and the Issue of the Bob in Modern China." *Fashion Theory* 1, no. 4 (1997): 353–65.
Sun Wanqun. "Chongsu nüxingmei de kanke zhi lu" ("The Rough and Bumpy Road toward a Remolding of Female Beauty"), *Zhongguo funü* (February 1992).
Susman, Warren. *Culture as History: The Transformation of American Society in the Twentieth Century*. New York: Pantheon, 1984.
Tsui, Christine. *China Fashion: Conversations with Designers*. Oxford: Berg Publishers, 2010.
Tu Wei-ming. "Cultural China: The Periphery as the Center." *Daedalus* 120, no. 2 (Spring 1991): 1–32.
Turner, Bryan S. *The Body and Society: Explorations in Social Theory*. London: SAGE, 1996.
Vatikiotis, Michael. "Family Matters: Modern Day Tensions Strain Southeast Asia's Social Fabric." *Far Eastern Economic Review* (August 1, 1996): 38–42.
Viroli, Maurizio. *For Love of Country: An Essay on Patriotism and Nationalism*. New York: Oxford University Press, 1997.
Wacker, Gudrun. *Werbung in der VR China (1979–1989): Entwicklung, Theorie, Probleme (Advertising in the People's Republic of China: Developments, Theories, Problems)*. Hamburg: Institut fur Asienkunde, 1991.
Wadler, Joyce. *Liaison*. New York: Bantam Books, 1993.
Wang Hui. "Bianzhe qianyan" (Editor's foreword). In idem and Yu Guoliang, eds., *Jiushi niandai de "houxue" lunzheng* ("The 1990s Debates on 'Post-isms'"). Hong Kong: Xianggang Zhongwen daxue, 1998: v–vii.
Wang Jian. "Crossing the River by Feeling the Stone: An Exploratory Study of the Process and Impact of Government Regulation of Foreign Advertising in the Chinese Market." Paper presented at the Asian Advertising and Media Conference, Hong Kong University, April 1998.
Wang Jing. *Brand New China: Advertising, Media, and Commercial Culture*. Cambridge, MA: Harvard University Press, 2008.

Wang Jing. "*He shang* and the Paradoxes of Chinese Enlightenment." *Bulletin of Concerned Asian Scholars* 23, no. 3 (July–September 1991): 23–33.

Wang Shaoguang. "The Politics of Private Time: Leisure Patterns in Urban China." In *Urban Spaces in China: The Potential for Autonomy and Community in Post-Mao China*, edited by Deborah S. Davis, Richard Kraus, Barry Naughton, and Elizabeth J. Perry, 149–72. Cambridge: Cambridge University Press, 1995.

Wang Xiong. "Hua! Jingren de xuesheng xiaofeichao" ("Alarming Trends in School Children's Consumption). *Caifeng* no. 2 (1993).

Wang Yonghua. "Wo diyici huazhuang zai riben" ("The First Time I Used Make-up Was in Japan"). *Zhongguo funü* (October 1993): 29.

Wang Zheng. *Never Forget National Humiliation: Historical Memory in Chinese Politics and Foreign Relations*. Columbia University Press, 2012.

Wang Zheng. "Gender, Employment and Women's Resistance." In *Chinese Society: Change, Conflict and Resistance*, edited by Elisabeth J. Perry and Mark Selden, 158–182. London: RoutledgeCurzon, 2003.

Wehrfritz, George. "A Chinese New Deal." *Newsweek* 116, issue 5991 (August 21, 1995): 5.

Wen Hua. *Buying Beauty: Cosmetic Surgery in China*. Hong Kong: Hong Kong University Press, 2013.

Wen Jie. "Nüxingde qingchun jiazhi hezai" (Of What Does the Value of Female Youth Consist?). Under the heading "Guanyu 'qingchun fan' de huati" (About 'Eating from the Ricebowl of Youth'). *Zhongguo funü* (January 1994): 11.

White, Gordon. *Riding the Tiger: The Politics of Economic Reform in Post-Mao China*. Stanford, CA: Stanford University Press, 1993.

Wilk, Richard. "Connections and Contradictions: From the Crooked Tree Cashew Queen to Miss World Belize." In *Beauty Queens on the Global Stage: Gender Contests and Power*, edited by Ballerino Cohen, Colleen, Richard Wilk, and Beverly Stoeltje, 217–32. New York: Routledge, 1996.

Williams, Maria. "'Face' Takes on New Meaning in Asian Ads." A*sian Advertising and Marketing* (July 1991).

Williamson, Judith. *Decoding Advertisements: Ideology and Meaning in Advertising*. New York; London: Marion Boyars Publishers, 1994.

Wilson, Verity. "Dress and the Cultural Revolution." In *China Chic: East Meets West,* edited by Valerie Steele and John S. Major, 167–86. New Haven, CT: Yale University Press, 1999.

Winship, Janice. *Inside Women's Magazines*. New York: Pandora, 1987.

Winship, Janice. "'Options—For the Way You Want to Live Now,' or a Magazine for Superwoman." *Theory, Culture & Society* 1 no. 3 (January 1983): 44–65.

Wu Jian*yuan. Chinese Fashion: From Mao to Now*. Oxford: Berg, 2009.

Xiao Ping. 1991. "Xiandai nüxing mei zhi wo jian" ("My Views on the Good Qualities of Modern Women"), *Zhongguo funü* (September 1991).

"Xinde nüxing yu xinde shidai" ("New Women, New Times"). *Zhongguo funü* (December 1991).

Xu, Ben. "Disan shijie piping' zai dangjin zhongguo de chujing" ("The predicament of Third World criticism in China today"). *Ershiyi shiji* (*Twenty-First Century*) 27, 16–27, 1995.

Yang, Mayfair Mei-hui. "From Gender Erasure to Gender Difference: State Feminism, Consumer Sexuality, and Women's Public Sphere in China." In *Spaces of Their Own: Women's Public Sphere in Transnational China*, edited by Mayfair Mei-hui Yang, 35–67. Minneapolis: University of Minnesota Press, 1999.

Yang, Mayfair Mei-hui. "Mass Media and Transnational Subjectivity in Shanghai: Notes on (Re)Cosmopolitanism in a Chinese Metropolis." In *Ungrounded Empires: The Cultural Politics of Modern Chinese Transnationalism*, edited by Aihwa Ong and Donald Noninim, 287–322. New York: Routledge, 1997.

Yao Fuyou. "Nürende rou" ("The Softness of Women"). *Hunyin yu jiating* (October 1993).

Yatsko, Pamela. "Inside Looking Out: Books and TV Dramas about Life Overseas Reflect Existing Chinese Biases." *Far Eastern Economic Review* 159, no. 15 (April 11, 1996): 58.

Yatsko, Pamela. "Pleasure and Profit." *Far Eastern Economic Review* (December 1998).

"Yazhou nüxing xiankuang diaocha dagongkai" ("An Investigation into the Current Situation for Asian Women Made Public"). *Nong* (February 1994): 149–52.

"Yiyan nan jinde" ("It Is Hard to Explain in Just a Few Words"). *Nüxing Yanjiu* (July 1993).

Yu Dafu. "Chenlun" ("Sinking"). *Chaungzao jikan* (*Creation Quarterly*) 1, no. 1 (October 1921).

Yu Xuejun. "Government Policies Toward Advertising in China (1979–1989)." *International Communication Gazette* 48, no. 1 1991): 17-30.

Yu Yan. "Nüren de huazhuang" ("Women's Make-up"). *Hunyin yu jiating* (February 1996).

Zha, Jianying. *China Pop: How Soap Operas, Tabloids, and Bestsellers are Transforming a Culture*. New York: The New Press, 1995.

Zhang Ailing. *Hong meigui yu bai meigui* (*Red Rose, White Rose*). Guangzhou: Huacheng chubanshe, 1996.

Zhang Longxi. *The Tao and the Logos: Literary Hermeneutics, East and West*. Durham, NC: Duke University Press, 1992.

Zhang Shuguang. "Yizhong zhanxin de tidai" (A Brand New Replacement) Under the heading "Guanyu 'qingchun fan' de huati: laizi duzhe de shengiyn" (About 'Eating the Fruits of Youth': voices from the readers). *Zhongguo funü* (January 1994): 23.

Zhang Xudong. *Postsocialism and Cultural Politics: China in the Last Decade of the Twentieth Century.* Durham, NC: Duke University Press, 2008.

Zhang Xudong. "Nationalism, Mass Culture, and Intellectual Strategies in Post-Tiananmen China." *Social Text*, no. 55 (Summer 1998): 109–40.

Zhang Xudong. *Chinese Modernism in the Era of Reform: Cultural Fever, Avant-garde Fiction, and the New Chinese Cinema*. Durham, NC: Duke University Press, 1997.

Zhang Yunjie. "Wo kan yangniu yu zhongguo guniang" ("Looking at Chinese and Western Young Women.") *Zhonguo funü* (June 1995): 47.

Zhao Bin. "Consumerism, Confucianism, Communism: Making Sense of China Today." *New Left Review* 1, no. 222 (1997): 43–59.

Zhao Bin and Graham Murdock. "Young Pioneers: Children and the Making of Chinese Consumerism." *Cultural Studies* 10, no. 2 (1996): 201–17.

Zhao Jianhua. *The Chinese Fashion Industry: An Ethnographic Approach*. London: Bloomsbury Academic, 2013.

Zhao Yiheng. "'Houxue' yu Zhongguo xin baoshou zhuyi" (Post-isms and Chinese neo-conservatism). *Ershiyi shiji* (Twenty-first Century) 27 (February 1995): 4–15.

Zhao Yuezhi. *Media, Market, and Democracy in China: Between the Party Line and the Bottom Line*. Urbana: University of Illinois Press, 1998.

Zhong Xueping. *Masculinity Besieged?: Issues of Modernity and Male Subjectivity in Chinese Literature of the Late Twentieth Century*. Durham, NC: Duke University Press, 2000.

"Zhongshi shenghuo fangshi de biange" ("Emphasize Changes in Life Styles"). *Renmin Ribao* (October 12, 1984).

Zhou Fanlin. "Hei fuse ren de meihua jiqiao" ("Beauty Techniques for Dark-Skinned People"). *Nüyou jinghuaben C* (no date): 99.

Žižek, Slavoj. "Courtly Love, or Woman as Thing." In *The Žižek Reader*, edited by Elizabeth Wright and Edmond Wright, 148–73. Oxford: Blackwell Publishers, 1999.

Žižek, Slavoj. *The Plague of Fantasies*. London; New York: Verso, 1997.

Žižek, Slavoj. *The Metastasis of Enjoyment: Six Essays on Women and Causality*. London; New York: Verso, 1994.

Žižek, Slavoj. "In his bold gaze my ruin is writ large." In *Everything You Always Wanted to Know About Lacan: (But Were Afraid to Ask Hitchcock)*, edited by Slavoj Žižek, 211–72. London; New York: Verso, 1992.

Žižek, Slavoj. *For They Know Not What They Do: Enjoyment as a Political Factor*. London: Verso, 1991.

Index

About the Author

Perry Johansson teaches contemporary China and Sino-American relations at Hong Kong Baptist University. He has been a visiting scholar at Columbia University and a senior research fellow at the National University of Singapore. Among his recent publications is *Saluting the Yellow Emperor: A Case of Swedish Sinography* (2012). At the moment he is working on a world history of the Vietnam War protests and a biography of Jan Myrdal.

Lightning Source UK Ltd.
Milton Keynes UK
UKOW02n1021191015

260893UK00001B/62/P

9 780739 192627